Brad Troemel

Peer
Pressure

Essays on the Internet
by an Artist on the Internet

LINK Editions

Domenico Quaranta, *In Your Computer*, 2011
Valentina Tanni, *Random*, 2011
Miltos Manetas, *In My Computer – Miltos Manetas*, 2011
Gene McHugh, *Post Internet*, 2011
Domenico Quaranta (ed.), *Collect the WWWorld. The Artist as Archivist in the Internet Age*, 2011. Exhibition Catalogue. Texts by Josephine Bosma, Gene McHugh, Joanne McNeil, Domenico Quaranta
Brad Troemel, *Peer Pressure*, 2011

Brad Troemel
Peer Pressure

Publisher: LINK Editions, Brescia 2011
www.linkartcenter.eu

This work is licensed under the Creative Commons Attribution-NonCommercial-ShareAlike 3.0 Unported License. To view a copy of this license, visit http://creativecommons.org/licenses/by-nc-sa/3.0/ or send a letter to Creative Commons, 171 Second Street, Suite 300, San Francisco, California, 94105, USA.

Printed and distributed by: Lulu.com
www.lulu.com

ISBN 978-1-4709-1561-2

for Nicolas Djandji

«*Everybody does have a book in them, but in most cases that's where it should stay.*»

_ *Christopher Hitchens*

Brad Troemel makes and writes about art on the internet. His writing has been featured in magazines and books. His art has been featured in galleries and sometimes even museums. He has earned two degrees from prestigious American art schools. He currently lives in a city full of diverse cultures and complicated intellectuals. Friend request or e-mail him, he'd be happy to talk to you. http://bradtroemel.com/

Contents

Brad is a Mod – by Eva and Franco Mattes 1

Introduction 5

What Relational Aesthetics Can Learn From 4Chan 9

The GIF's Obsession With Compression 19

Why No Serious? A Case for Idealism in an Era of Constant Irony 25

From Clubs to Affinity: The Decentralization of Art on the Internet 33

Provocative Materiality in the Valley of Death 47

The Many Faces of Tumblr 55

Making The Best of a Permanent Pay Freeze 61

The Emergence of Dual Sites 67

New Productive Systems 71

Screens on Screens (Ben Schumacher) 85

Why You Should Make Yourself Someone Else Online 91

Tsimulacrum 99

In Response to 'Dispersion' by Seth Price 103

The Minor League 111

The Wealth of Pointlessness 119

Friend Request From My Mom 125

Brad is a Mod

One night we ran into a text by this guy Brad Troemel titled "What Relational Aesthetics Can Learn From 4Chan?" and it kept us awake for hours. It was exactly what we were thinking when we made many of our works, but we didn't know it. Unknown knowns? So who the hell was this Brad Troemel that could read our mind?

Right than we got invited to a dinner in New York by artist Constant Dullaart. We went there and apparently it was all people from the art world. We didn't know anybody, so it was nice but also a bit embarrassing. The one thing that made our dinner was a guy at the other end of the long table. Eva and I kept looking at him and laughin 'cause he totally looked like a friend of ours, Matteo Erenbourg from the group Alterazioni Video. Matteo is a very funny and interesting fellow, so we took a liking to this guy, even if we had no idea who he was. After the dinner we all went to another bar, a fancy one with music. We ended up sitting by the Matteo look-alike guy. And than something odd happened: trying to be unnoticed we took out our little bottle of whiskey, that we always keep for situations like this one (expensive New York bars) and right at the same time this guy was drawing out from below the table his own little bottle of whiskey. Lulz ensued. Who was this dude who totally looked like a friend and was drinking from a hidden bottle like us? Brad Troemel, of course. We got along right away.

What we love about his texts is that despite being one of the most up-to-date writers we know, he's not post-modern, he is a modernist, he claims his theories like manifestos, not much room for tongue-in-cheeks and winkings, just look at the video of his lecture Free Art, he is closer to a Net-Marinetti than to an academic.

Reading Brad we started noticing a difference that is becoming more and more relevant, the difference between artists using the internet as a huge free mine of images and ideas that can be scavenged, modified, printed, sculpted, raped, sold, bought... and artists who also give something back to the internet, who consider it their place and time, their natural audience, and from the internet get their pleasure & pain. Brad belongs to this second group. He gives back way more than he takes. The internet approves.

So, we've been asked to write an introduction to Brad's book, we never wrote an introduction to any book, and we were never ourselves introduced to Brad, we just happened to pull out our hidden bottles of booze right at the same time. Plus, Brad puts his writings and his art up on the internet right away, he doesn't wait for galleries or publishers, he goes straight to his readers, without introduction, without mediators, so why would he care for an introduction now?

Eva and Franco Mattes aka 0100101110101101.ORG
New York, October 2011

Introduction

I used to really hate art objects and the buildings that housed them. This was because I thought they were unnecessarily exclusive, that only certain people could interact with them in certain places at certain times. To a degree, I still believe this. It was because I wanted to reach the maximum number of people that I always put everything I made on the internet as soon as possible after I completed it. I came to realize this was a somewhat exclusionary idea too, that only allowing things to exist in digital form precluded a number of interactions people could have with my writing. This point was made especially apparent in graduate school, when I would be assigned hundreds of pages of reading a week and it became difficult for me to stare at a computer screen for that long. Owning a desktop, it also meant I could only read at school in my studio. I started printing the assigned books and essays out so I could travel with them and mark them up as I went along. This worked really well for me, and it made sense that other people might want to be given the option to read my own writing on paper. If not, they can always download it for free online.

My friends say I have a tendency of peer pressuring them at parties and being notoriously aggressive in art school critiques. I recognize these tendencies persist through the writing in this book for better or worse; each essay is an impassioned description or prescription to understand the digital space we inhabit differently. All of these essays were written about subject matters that were very current at the time – galleries that had started only weeks earlier, types of websites just springing into existence, freshly minted memes. For this reason I feel I'm always speaking to a very selective group of people when I publish writing. Fewer people are aware of or care about Productive Systems, for instance, than if I were to examine a topic as broad and old as American Modernism. It's also because I write about things that are still being decided by an intimate group of artists that my writing often attracts so much comment thread flaming (a fact I'm still getting used to).

I write with certainty as a counter-weight to the total cluelessness I feel when making art. Most of the projects I produce involve some element of online group participation, user generated content, or collaboration with people who are infinitely more knowledgeable than me in the technical workings of programming. In several instances I've had entire blogs and projects deleted from the internet overnight. Some of my projects have surged with hundreds of participants while others have been abandoned by their users almost as quickly as they started. I never really know what I'm getting into when I start these things, I only have an idea of the kind of social structure I want to encourage.

It's necessary for me to have an open mind when publishing art because I can only expect to be disappointed if my hopes for a specific result are too firm. Writing is different because of its reflective nature. "This thing happened (however recently) and here's what I think of it." I suppose there's a risk of sticking your neck out too soon through writing as well (of not knowing what people will say or do in response), but that's probably why I like doing it.

Brad Troemel, New York, October 2011

What Relational Aesthetics Can Learn From 4Chan

Is it still necessary to define art by intent and context? The gallery world would have us believe this to be the case, but the internet tells a more mutable story. Contrary to the long held belief that art needs intent and context, I suggest that if we look outside of galleries, we'll find the actions, events and people that create contemporary art with or without the art world's label.

Over the past 20 years, the theory Relational Aesthetics (referred to in this essay as RA) has interpreted social exchanges as an art form. Founding theoretician Nicolas Bourriaud describes this development as "a set of artistic practices that take as their theoretical and practical point of departure the whole of human relations and their social context" [1]. In reality, art erroneously known to typify RA's theorization hasn't strayed far from the model of the 1960's Happening, an event beholden to the conventions of the gallery and the direction of its individual creator. In her essay "Antagonism and Relational Aesthetics", Claire Bishop describes Rirkrit Tiravanija's dinners as events circumscribed in advance, using their location as a crutch to differentiate the otherwise ordinary action of eating a meal as art [2]. A better example of the theory of RA succinctly put into action can be seen in anonymous group activities on the internet, where people form relations and meaning without hierarchy.

Started in 2003, 4Chan.org is one such site, and host to 50 image posting message boards (though one board in particular, simply titled '/b/', is responsible for originating many of the memes we use to burn our free time). The site's 700,000 daily users post and comment in complete anonymity; a bathroom-stall culture generating posts that alternate between comedic brilliance, virulent hate and both combined. Typically, the content featured is a NSFW intertextual gangbang of obscure references and in-jokes where images are created, remixed, popularized and forgotten about in a matter of hours. 4Chan keeps no permanent record of itself, making an in the moment experience the allure of participation. For all of the memes that have leaked into our inbox from it, 4Chan maintains a language, ethics and set of activities that would be incomprehensible to the unfamiliar viewer. Induction to /b/'s world is not fortified and understanding it merely requires Google searching its litany of acronymated terms or lurking regularly enough to find out for yourself.

"It is up to us as beholders of art to bring [unforeseen associations] to light, [...] to judge artworks in terms of the relations they produce in the specific contexts they inhabit", concludes Bourriaud in his 2001 book, *Postproduction* [3]. One of the unforeseen relationships he mentions is that of the contemporary artist and contributive internet surfer (the kind of Photoshop bandit you can find on /b/). Bourriaud understands each as methodological equals, calling them "semionauts". He uses this term to define those who create pathways through culture by reorganizing history to bring forward new ideas [4]. In a digital environment equally defined by information categorizing and shopping, a case for surfing-as-art neatly falls between two historical precedents: Duchamp's specification-as-art and 1980's artists' (such as Jeff Koons, Sherrie Levine, or Haim Steinbach) interest in consumption-as-art. Surfing-as-art and RA both enact Peter Bürger's description of the avant-garde's intention to merge everyday life with the aesthetic realm.

Marcin Ramocki's essay "Surfing Clubs: organized notes and comments" describes the rapid conversations on group posting websites using jpgs, gifs, video, links, and text as a material:

> The older the club the more convoluted the semiotics of communication between surfers becomes. This communication entails posting organized content by a challenger, and a decoding of it by other participants, who respond with a posting where both syntagms and paradigms of the challenge post are identified and playfully manipulated. [5]

The medium, practice and logic of surf clubs outlined in Ramocki's essay matches 4Chan's /b/ message board identically, though the circumstances are obviously different. While /b/ anonymously concerns itself with people and events popularized on the internet, the individuals who manage surf clubs have social and professional connections to the art world, making their primary point of reference art historical. Reference should not be the sole criteria for understanding surfing-as-art, however. Ramocki, like Bourriaud, premises his belief in surfing-as-art not on the type of allusions made in content, but on the production method of a post and its network environment. Both describe this environment as continuously active, altering or re-contextualizing information and making it public with hope for further use by peers.

With this condition in mind, it's fair to call /b/ a massive surf club whose conceptual language is determined by those without connections to the art world or the need for validation from it. As artist and blogger Eryk Salvaggio puts it, "The net can't handle the pretense of art, or anything that seems manufactured, because it has a keen bullshit mechanism." [6] Though /b/ doesn't need us, contemporary art does need a dose of /b/'s refined understanding of actively anonymous group creation for us to advance the "bullshit" we cherish.

The notion of ongoing use in surf clubs is also fundamental to RA's attempt to create an art that takes place through the continuous social interactions participants have within an environment. Ramocki describes surf clubs as more than a dump site for disparate images, but as a location where highly specific visual languages are formed and conversed in. This corresponds with Bourriaud's description of the future of Relational art:

> artists intuitive relationship with art history is now going beyond what we call "the art of appropriation," which naturally infers an ideology of ownership, and moving toward a culture of use of forms, a culture of constant activity of signs based on a collective ideal: sharing. [7]

From this quote we can draw another relationship: /b/ and other surf clubs are digital examples of Relational Aesthetics, art forms that rely on social interaction and feedback to take place. But before /b/ can totally fall under the hood of RA, there is one last hurdle in aligning it with Bourriaud's theory. The book *Relational Aesthetics* reflected Bourriaud's distrust for technology, a feeling so deep he even criticized automatic public toilets as instruments that distance the public from itself. Bourriaud saw the 1990's generation's drive to initiate an art consisting of intimate human relations as a reaction to the disembodying effects of the digital age.

These theories are now out of date. Understanding our only 'real' relations as those that occur through physical encounters becomes arbitrary when considering the behavioral and situational norms each physical encounter presents. Each of these norms acts as an intermediary between others and ourselves (though some would argue these norms do not regulate, but *are* our personalities). Like the digital world, physical interaction is full of socially bound interfaces, operating methods that determine the substance of relationships. As any millennial can attest, the idea that there is an in-person 'real' version of you that comprises your full identity and an online personage that bears no impact on your 'real' self, isn't an accurate description of contemporary life. The inclusion of digital sites of interaction as a development of Relational Aesthetics is an idea not so strange considering the method's practitioners' past interest in the economics of mass exchange, intermediary points of being during travel and the collision of global cultures.

An expansion into the digital world could also help clarify RA in practice; it is a theory with an open disdain for art's commodification, though is often exhibited within the shelter of an art institution. This discrepancy was best articulated, oddly enough, by dealer Gavin Brown, sharply saying in an interview with the BBC:

> Don't you think that if you wanted to look at the possibilities of an art that's theoretical horizons encompass the realm of human interactions in a social context, wouldn't you want to just go out and meet people and have a good life? I mean, to me it seems as though a lot of this work is made by people who are scared to live life in the first place – incredibly unradical people [8] who play a game of a radical life in the safe confines of some Kunsthalle or other museum in Germany or France. [9]

Despite Bourriaud's interest in collaborative art making, his theory's purest realization has been put on hold by institutions that must place emphasis on individual creators to maintain their financial well-being. While inside of a Liam Gillick exhibit, have you ever forgot that you were attending a Liam Gillick exhibit? I haven't. Ending the viewer/creator dichotomy requires no less than the end of the art-star system and a participation format that makes room for the errors inherent in participants' free will. In his essay "Postchronist Manifestation", Dominick Chen states: "as long as there exists an asymmetry (or distance) between producer and receiver, the modality of cultural production would inevitably lead back to a religious power structure." [10]

An art of Relational Aesthetics "far from the classical mythology of the solitary effort" [11] would be anonymously produced and give all participants the greatest degree of choice possible when determining the course of their own experience. Here we arrive again at 4Chan.

In addition to the constantly evolving visual and textual language on 4Chan's message boards, there is another /b/ activity that exemplifies group production in line with RA's theory. These activities are called 'raids' – projects where a person or institution is chosen and a mass of anonymous people contribute to bringing on the manipulation of its digital existence.

While a surf club may screen capture and edit material in Photoshop to post to their board, /b/'s raids are concerned with bringing on an evolving change in the source itself, not a visualized hypothetical. Surf-clubs have a Relational structure of communication among members, but they still maintain the individual creation of static art within a designated space. In contrast, raids are a breach of boundaries – a way of altering the work's 'real life'. William S. Burroughs' proposition that art manifest itself ("What if a painting of a bomb exploded in a gallery?") is fitting for raids [12]. These site-specific alterations may take place through cracking passwords, using the open editing features on a website like Wikipedia, or hacking. Sometimes they even take place in person.

Raids have no leaders and the course of their action is decided by the collective will(s) of all participants. Without a direct chain of command, a raid is an event constantly in flux. They may end before they even start or begin with one plan of action and later morph into many splintering reactions. A raid's anti-hierarchical fragmentation is similar to the antagonism Claire Bishop describes in "Antagonism and Relational Aesthetics". Separate from the temporary microtopias attempted by some RA artists, Bishop calls the social works of art that reveal natural oppositions between participants an example of relational antagonism. She explains that this art making is a way of "exposing that which is repressed in sustaining the semblance of harmony." [13]

Antagonism is a byproduct of free choice and speech – an inefficient but necessary way of relating if a project wishes to remain as open as possible. 4Chan users tend to value personal liberty above all, making the prime targets of their raids people or companies who engage in censorship or moral zealotry [14]. Disgust for authority is so engrained in /b/'s culture of anonymity that users who attempt to demand raids for their own personal gain have became the target of backlash attacks themselves. While some group interventions are petty, others are thought provoking and intelligently executed, like 2009's mARBLECAKEALSOTHEGAME raid, which is /b/'s finest work yet.

When TIME Magazine offered 4Chan's founder, m00t, as a candidate for 2009's 100 Most Influential People of the Year online readership poll, /b/ wasted no time launching an attack to propel him to the top spot. The resulting campaign included likely thousands of participants' manual labor, the creation and dispersion of sophisticated ballot-stuffing software programs and several strategic changes [15] in online manipulation methods from March to April of 2009. m00t not only took first place, but all of the top 21 people listed in the poll were intentionally ordered in such a way that their first names spelled out a secret message: 'mARBLE CAKE ALSO THE GAME'[16]. 'Marble cake' is alternately described as the name of the chat room where the anti-Scientology raid Project Chanology was born, or as an unsanitary sex act. 'The game' is an inside joke that requires you to not utter or think of it to be able to win. You mostly likely just lost the game.

The mARBLE CAKE raid was a reflexive commentary on and literal revision of whom the public thought they voted to be the most powerful that year. The ranked influence of the names listed in the top 21 become subservient to the order of /b/'s encrypted message. This echoes the commonly launched criticism of TIME's yearly "Influential" issue that many of the people included are merely entertaining figureheads or patsies who act at the behest of even more powerful, discrete interests. In addition to this, the raid is a work of Relational Aesthetics. Just as the empty bottles left over from Rirkrit Tiravanija's meals are later used as sculptures, the resulting alteration of TIME's poll became a digital monument to /b/'s successfully group-orchestrated intervention. What we witness by looking at the mARBLE CAKE raid is the result of a group of computer programmers who used their knowledge to make a mockery of a flawed media structure without retaining individual credit for themselves. With this equally creditless result, I'm reminded of the symmetrical creativity Dominick Chen calls for in his essay "Postchronist Manifestation". Chen situates Relational Aesthetics as the second to most current form of art making in history. The newest, he claims, is as-of-yet unmade, though differs from RA in that it is created and interpreted collectively without hierarchy. This 'new' form of art does not exist inside of traditional institutions and confronts the conditions of its participants' lives within their own environment.

What Chen describes is in fact Relational Aesthetics as ideally theorized by Bourriaud, highlighting the contradiction between the reality of RA's art-star-filled, institutionally reified present incarnation and the hope for an emancipatory future inherent in RA's theory. Chen calls this 'new' form of art 'X' but he might as well have named it /b/.

2010. Originally published in *Art Fag City*.

[1] Nicolas Bourriaud, *Relational Aesthetics*, Les Press Du Reel, France 1998, p. 113.
[2] Clare Bishop, "Antagonism and Relational Aesthetics", in *October 110*, Fall 2004, p. 69.
[3] Nicolas Bourriaud, *Postproduction*, Lukas and Sternberg, New York 2002, p. 94.
[4] Ibid., p. 18
[5] Marcin Ramocki, "Surf Clubs: organized notes and comments", Self published, May 27, 2008, p. 5.
[6] Comment by Eryk Salvaggio on Rhizome.org discussion board, May 12, 2008. Online at www.rhizome.org/discuss/view/37290.
[7] Bourriaud 2002, p. 4.
[8] It should be mentioned that his gallery, Gavin Brown Enterprise represents several Relational artists, calling into question whether this answer was hypocritically sincere, ironic or Sophist.
[9] BBC News, *"Relational Art: Is it an Ism?"*, 2004. www.ubu.com/film/relational.html.
[10] Dominick Chen, "Postchronist Manifestation", in Geert Lovink, Sabine Neiderer (Eds.), *Video Vortex Reader. Responses to Youtube*, Institute of Network Cultures, Amsterdam 2008, p. 74.
[11] Bourriaud 2002, p. 10.
[12] William S. Burroughs, "The Fall of Art", in *The Adding Machine: Selected Essays*, Arcade Publishing, 1993, p. 62.
[13] Bishop 2004, p. 79.
[14] Julian Dibbell describes 4Chan's ethos as "radically authorless, furiously remixed and compulsively serious" while imagining their antithesis as "a strictly disciplined, hierarchical organization founded on the exact reproduction of relentlessly earnest, fiercely copyright-protected words". In Julian Dibbell, "The Assclown Offensive: How to Enrage the Church of Scientology", in Wired, September 21, 2009.

Online at www.wired.com/culture/culturereviews/magazine/17-10/mf_chanology?currentPage=all.

[15] Because the poll took account of both the number of votes and the average rating of influence (a number up to 100 at best), the ballot stuffing software distributed among participants needed to take use complicated algorithms to insure each of the 21 names would stay high or low enough on the list for the mARBLE CAKE message to be spelled properly. As the raid continued, TIME caught on to these attempts and upped their security measures. Throughout the month the mARBLECAKEALSOTHEGAME message became illegible many times, forcing raiders to adopt new methods to combat Captcha Codes and time restrictions. As the amount of manual labor increased, many lost interest in the project and moved on. Participants came and went all throughout the raid – free choice includes the possibility of refusal.

The GIF's Obsession With Compression

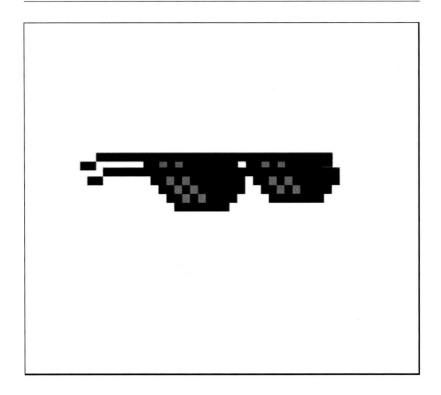

Compression is a process that aims for greater efficiency. Compression streamlines all that is 'unnecessary' by compacting a product to reveal only its most essential components. The compressed product's new, slender form allows it to be used, seen, transmitted or reproduced with greater ease than its previously bulky or complicated body. An argument can be made that whatever is able to be used with the *greatest* ease is that which has been functionally compressed to the fullest extent. The internet has compressed many things already previously compressed, creating objects both extremely heavy in connotations and extremely light at first appearance. Just as spoken language is a compression of lived experience, so too is the written word a compression of spoken language, and so too is net-speak an even further compression of all of these things. A smiley face emoticon is seen as a frivolous token of online chatter – unless you consider it the latest technologically-bound stop in the progression of humanity's desire to articulate joy, then it becomes something a bit more complex.

Ideally, compression does not delete information or material but conceals it within itself, making all hidden components readily accessible should the person interacting with a compressed product wish to unzip or re-expand its contents. Of course not all methods of compression lend themselves to different subjects equally well. Compressing a cat's personal space for plane travel in the manner a watermelon is compressed for a fruit smoothie would be disastrous. As art is digitally mediated, so too does it become materially and experientially compressed. This inevitably creates a dichotomy of quality of experience versus ease of access. Positions over which or if any forms of compression should be applicable to art arise. People against art's digital mediation claim it to be a vulgar distortion of experiential affect and a forcible removal of aesthetics. People in support of art's digital mediation point to the way it opens previously rigid institutional and architectural boundaries of participation, allowing an exponentially larger number of viewers to become aware of and join in art's discourse. Though in the past I have favored the latter of these two positions, I wonder if such distinctions are quite so black and white. For instance, what role do formats that are native to digital viewing play in this conversation? They cannot be judged against the backdrop of a formerly physical existence but must be critically analyzed unto themselves. One such example that comes to mind is the artistic GIF.

The general popularity of GIFs is easy to understand. They're simple to make, playfully animated, cross-browser compatible and fun to watch. GIFs have a history in both vernacular net use and internet art, as well as a history at the intersection between the two. As a visual medium, GIFs are caught in a space sandwiched between still images and film. Arguably, all film is just a rapid procession of still images, but while film conceals this fact the GIF often reveals which frames comprise it by plodding through them in a manner similar to stop animation during the process of loading. GIFs lend themselves to subject matters that may be quickly summed up in the fewest number of frames possible or to content that has no beginning or end and may be understood equally well starting from any moment in a brief, looping format. As writer Jonah Weiner says in his essay "Christina Hendricks on an Endless Loop" [1]:

> [Many GIFs] are built around the payoff moments of *Did you see that?*-style viral videos. These GIFs are structured like jokes, with the barest minimum of set-up... They get to the point instantaneously, and at the exact moment when one feels the impulse to rewind and watch the climax again, the loop restarts right where it should... Like an enhanced bumper sticker or T-shirt, the GIF offers a pithy, punchy means for self-expression.

This kind of self-expression is largely conversational; on message boards the GIF provides an excellent way of responding to a previous poster in a direct manner that transcends the time necessary to read and decode language. The lure of using a GIF is that it is designed not to be poured over as an individual object of dense decoding but to be seen, to trigger an immediate response, and be moved on from. On the subject of the GIF's accepted immediacy, writer Joshua Kopstein states in "The GIF That Keeps On GIFing" [2]:

> Human memory is intimately tied to isolated moments in time. According to the Atkinson-Shifrin model – the same one that divided human memory into long-term, short-term and sensory – most of the things we experience are not committed to long-term memory beyond a few select moments. So it makes sense that we've embraced GIFs as these suspended moments in time, looping only the information necessary to conjure a particular emotion or memory.

The GIF's straightforward looping mechanism revels in its own simplicity and the manner in which it professes to be nothing more profound than what 3 seconds of your time can possibly allow for as a work of visual art. In an online environment that exalts immediacy and ease of use, the GIF is not a fetishization of the past or Web 1.0 culture – as many have argued – but a fetishization of the internet's propensity for compressing information to the furthest degree possible. In a world of Macbook Airs, external hard drives the size of a thumb, and 140 character limits on textual communication, the GIF is a suitable alternative for those who can't quite make it through a 2 minute Youtube video without advancing forward to the 1:00 and 1:30 minute markers after the first 10 seconds prove too dull for viewing. The most crucial question for artists to ask in response to the GIF's obsession with compression is whether the GIF is a true harbinger of conceptual efficiency or an ornamental novelty of its own lightness?

GIFs do not require an embedded player to be viewed and have remained functional throughout many shifts in applicable file formats on the web. This longevity and uniform accessibility has lead many to characterize the GIF as a file format as democratic as the internet purportedly aspires to be. However, unlike Hito Steyerl's accurately egalitarian description of the *poor image* [3], the low visual quality of a GIF is not a result of pirated mass reproduction or individuals cycling images through a slew of diverse copying and transfer methods. Instead, the GIF's limited capacity for narrative and often pixilated appearance is due to the increased bulk each frame adds to its total file size, subsequently slowing down the process of loading and viewing the larger the file gets. Without the external support of a video player, the GIF must behave as an image while appearing to be a video.

As a culturally distinct and informationally narrowed format, the content of an artistic GIF rarely strays far from the realm of the expected due to the inherently minimal range of visuals and narrative advancements it may include as a time-based medium. All forms of compression eventually meet their logical end, where whatever material was compressed is no longer able to be recovered in quite the same manner it previously existed, resulting in an unzipped product that appears to be a faint shadow of the dense form it once took. The fault of the artistic GIF is not that it has rendered conceptually rich subjects to a point incapable of being critically expanded upon with conceptual depth, but that the format itself is a censorship of an amount of information necessary to create ideologically rich narratives transcendent of their own interface. In a recent essay on the state of internet-informed art titled "Walking Free" [4], curator Lauren Cornell states:

> While the field of art online continues to thrive, art engaged with the internet does not need to exist there; because the internet is not just a medium, but also a territory populated and fought over by individuals, corporations, and governments; a communications tool; and a cultural catalyst.

The idea that art's subject matter need not address the same medium it assumes is an adequate description of a contemporary field of art making that has increasingly come to rely less on medium specificity for critical validation. As Cornell echoes, the best art on the internet or otherwise exceeds its own medium, inspiring realizations divorced from whatever it is being transmitting through. The GIF is indelibly and formally linked to the compressed boundaries of the file format that transmits it, allowing art viewers none of the suspension of disbelief necessary to think the GIF they are looking at is not, in fact, a GIF at any moment of their viewing. The solution to the artistic GIF's status as a pre-emptively self-referential medium would require it to betray its own maxim of economical viewing and transfer. Impossibly, this would force the GIF to aesthetically become, in a word, *inefficient*. Some problems just can't be fixed. The artistic GIF will have to deal with it.

Written in 2011.

[1] Jonah Weiner, "Christina Hendricks on an Endless Loop. The glorious GIF renaissance", in *Slate,* October 14, 2010. Online at www.slate.com/articles/arts/culturebox/2010/10/christina_hendricks_on_an_endless_loop.html.
[2] Joshua Kopstein, "The GIF That Keeps On GIFing: Why Animated Images Are Still A Defining Part Of Our Internets", In *Motherboard*, November 19, 2010. Online at www.motherboard.tv/2010/11/19/the-gif-that-keeps-on-gifing-why-animated-images-are-still-a-defining-part-of-our-internets.
[3] Hito Steyerl, "In Defense of the Poor Image", in *e-flux magazine*, Issue 10, November 2010. Online at: www.e-flux.com/journal/view/94.
[4] Lauren Cornell, "Walking Free", in *Free*, exhibition catalogue, The New Museum, New York, October 20, 2010 ~ January 23, 2011. Online at www.newmuseum.org/free/#laurencornell.

Why No Serious?
A Case for Idealism in
an Era of Constant Irony

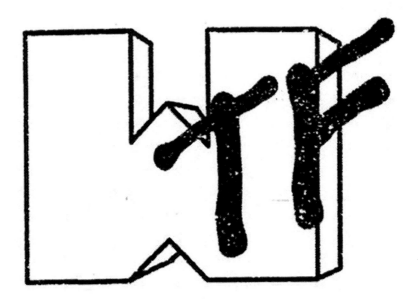

My generation is more ironic than any that has came before it. Maybe we're just coping with the difficulties of transitioning into a newly digitized social space. On the subject of British life in the wake of the industrial revolution, Clay Shirkey says:

> The transformation from rural to urban life was so sudden, and so wrenching, that the only thing society could do to manage was to drink itself into a stupor for a generation. The stories from that era are amazing – there were gin pushcarts working their way through the streets of London. [1]

This ubiquitous stupor feels familiar to me, as I surf from one faux-naïve website to the next or read my daily onslaught of jokey and intentionally misspelled Facebook commentary it becomes very apparent that I live in an environment of constant irony on the internet. As a regular user of irony myself, I don't want to quit it cold turkey. There are tons of great applications for irony – but the problem is when it becomes *constant*, when all dialogue is filtered through a single rhetorical device and when other expressive options – namely, the sincerity required by idealism – become demonized to the point of extinction. How did we, as a generation of artists and non-artists, get ourselves in to this mess and how can we climb out of the ironic hole we've fallen into? This writing is one attempt to promote the benefits of ideal convictions for artists and to explain how to be an idealist without reverting back to modernist ways of thinking.

Irony is a contradiction. What is ironic betrays itself to reveal its true nature. Irony can be manifested through a signifier displayed in a way that reflects oppositely of what is signified (a Red Sox logo turned blue), the signified contradicting its context (the unabashed kitsch of a dog made of flowers sitting in front of the Guggenheim Bilbao), or a plot where the audience is made aware of more about the narrative than the actors in it (classical theater). Irony can also be used as a way a for a speaker to appear as though she knows less than the viewer so to secretly guide her viewer down a path towards meaning (Socrates).

Irony has long been part of bohemian (read: hipster) cultures since the days when 19th century flaneurs would stroll through the streets of Paris with pet turtles on leashes. Of course the flaneur *knew* what he was doing, recognizing the absurdity of his actions and carried forth anyway as a self-aware spectacle. The joke was not on the man walking a turtle down a single block for an hour, but on the naïve person who thought the flaneur was mad. The square who conformed to normal walking speeds with her conventional pets was the butt of the joke.

Irony always requires some extra information to be understood, making it at odds with the supposedly self-evident nature of modern art, as championed by Abstract Expressionist painting and the similarly arch-modernist genre of Minimalism. When in 1961 Frank Stella described his works as "a flat surface with paint on it – nothing more", the nothingness to which he refers may be a negating acknowledgement of either figural representation or the incoming conceptualist notion that art act as a system for the creation of itself in the mind of its viewer. In this way conceptualism shares some basic similarities with irony – both are meant to enact awarenesses that transcend their signifiers alone.

It should be made clear that my generation did not inherit irony from Socrates, Sol Lewitt, or the flaneurs, and that our popular understanding of irony comes from the three figures that raised us – our parents, television and the internet.

Novelist Douglas Coupland used the term Generation X [2] to describe people born between 1961 and 1981 and who were the first to be raised in the Post Modern era – a generation my own parents are a part of. Unlike the uniformity and resolve of Baby Boomers to perpetually offer a group of late 1960's rock bands as the undisputed 'best ever', Gen X'ers had a harder time coming to a musical consensus, nit-picking at each other's taste in popular music across a variety of counter-slogans from "Disco Sucks" to "Punk is Dead" to the "death of hair metal" at the hands of grunge. In his writing *The Hipness Unto Death: Soren Kierkagaard and David Letterman – Ironic Apologists to Generation X*, Mark C. Miller [3] echoes this sentiment, saying about Gen X'ers:

> A trillion dollar debt is theirs to inherit, and Social Security is theirs to give but never to receive. They feel alienated and disillusioned, and are disparaged by the baby boomers with whom they so often feel at war... With more than half of them coming from divorced families, and with innumerable advertisements targeting their massive market demographic, they are cynical, wary, and apathetic... Generation X, suspicious and indifferent, needs nothing.

The one thing it turned out Generation X did want was MTV – a gift they passed on to us. Perhaps MTV was an easier pill for Gen X'ers to swallow because it was, at the time, one of the most sophisticated advertising mechanisms to have ever existed. In the documentary *Merchants of Cool* [4], Robert McChesney says:

> All of MTV is a commercial. That's all that MTV is. Sometimes it's an explicit advertisement paid for by a company to sell a product. Sometimes it's going to be a video by a music company there to sell music. Sometimes it's going to be the set that's filled with trendy clothes and stuff there to sell a look that will include products on that set. Sometimes it will be a show about an upcoming movie paid for by the studio (but you don't know it) to hype a movie coming out from Hollywood. There is no non-commercial part of MTV.

Banking on the first wholly Post Modern generation's belief in the death of isolationist originality in favor of multiple and fluid identities, companies like MTV were more than happy to take advantage of Gen X'ers unwillingness to commit to a single style or belief, actively accelerating the exposure and subsequent turn over rate of commercialized sub cultures at a pace more rapid than ever before all through televised media. The goal of this acceleration was to create a consumer environment so fast moving that even a momentary commitment to a shirt or band would be ridden with the self-doubt that another product would not only replace it, but demean all those who formerly associated with its predecessor. In a pop culture where the assumption of planned obsolescence has been engrained in every product mass marketed, irony serves as a way to simultaneously associate and distance one's self from all things in the same way companies promote both the success and failure of what they offer. The result of this in and out, yes and no, love and hate generational affair is the onset of *porous* identities. A porous identity can be understood as a person riddled with many holes of doubt and consumptive anxiousness waiting for admittedly temporary fixes to sooth the emptiness of a life without any firm conviction.

Porous identities were no match for the commercial internet, the fastest and latest in a long line of media projects designed to link the desires of consumers and the products of sellers in the most direct way possible. The internet – much like its users ironic disposition – is *constant* in many ways. It's constant in that its information is constantly moving and available, for one, but it's also constant in the way it attunes each of its users to their status as a consumptive agent from the moment you pay for wireless access, to the moment you log in to your data-mined e-mail account, to the never ending side bars and introductions full of advertising a viewer must endure to watch a single video. There is no escape from what is constant and it is here we arrive at a perfect storm for the permanently ironic person. At the intersecting lines of three things that all prize 'the new' at the cost of quickly moving trends planned for obsolescence (youth culture, the internet and contemporary art) internet art is a prime location for people of constantly ironic dispositions.

Used as a coping mechanism for the anxiety caused by rapid cultural turn over, constant irony is the reclamation of hopelessness or lack of idealistic creativity spoken through the voice of detached coolness. For artists, being constantly ironic is an effective deflection of one's own porosity because it provides the illusion you were too cunning to have ever wanted anything more solidified. At the peak of the artistic internet's speed is the image aggregating blog, a place where thousands of images can be circulated in a single week without any textual explanation. The irony here is an archival one; immense networks of divergent signifiers compete for attention and contradict one another in a process whereby the blog's poster is revealed to have an ever-increasing awareness of sub cultures and access to rare or unseen material. The turn over rate of subcultural awareness made public harkens back to MTV but is completed on an individual basis at light speed. While the digital liberation of images from traditional modes of authorship, context and property marks a seismic shift in visual culture, the full potential of this change remains unfulfilled. Willingness to politically or conceptually use images is stunted by a constantly ironic generation's aversion to anything even remotely resembling the monumentality of having a specified conviction. 'Meaning' is culled not on the basis of content's re-purposing but on the level of establishing personal brands for the all-aware bloggers. The constantly ironic digital populace outwardly believes in nothing more solidified than their last blog post, despite an addiction to proving they are aware of everything and everyone.

While the rise of a visually superficial internet art world is the result of constant irony, there is a more grave consequence concealed by how difficult it has come to be found on the internet. I am speaking of the disappearance of idealism, the most deep-rooted and alarming of developments to take place. The constant irony I speak of does not conceal idealism, but is a reactionary response to the compounding belief that political or artistic progress of any kind is unfeasible. In place of idealism's motivation for social change is inserted an infatuation with the self, a compulsion to maintain individual brands and invigorate one's own status in the attention economy of art online. The emptiness of an artistic life staked as a personal popularity campaign alone (occasionally interrupted by peer accolades or institutional recognition) is resounding, and leaves the constantly ironic individual in the doubled down position to embrace her own emptiness in an ironic fashion. Enter Andy Warhol's "I'm in it for the money." Empty because of irony, ironic because of emptiness. The cycle of addiction is self-perpetuating.

Artistic idealism is worth re-examining. The notion that ideals are never fully realized is absolutely true, so why have them at all? The answer to this question shares some aspects with the answer to the question, "Why make art?". Both art and ideals are impossible things; in the case of art it means to make the world seen, if only momentarily, in a way more critically accurate or beautiful than what we are accustom to seeing. Art is impossible because we may never see the entire world with perfect clarity forever due to a single project – art has a temporary affect. Ideals – the articulation of a utopic reality – also serve as a means to expand our continuum of the possible, if only to nudge us the furthest *toward* a utopic reality or to re-orient our expectations of what is possible. Only the most belligerent idealists seek to impose their utopic reality on all – a reality that would inevitably be hellish for many. Idealism can be contingent, limited to single causes or the creation of specific things – a more open system for the validation and dispersion of art, for example. Take for instance the most successful idealists of American politics in the last 30 years: Christian Fundamentalists and Neo Liberals. These idealist factions have forced politicians to slide increasingly towards the respective religious and corporatist extremes every election cycle despite never fully achieving a Christian or free marketed nation. When idealism is ardently and openly believed by a critical mass it is wildly successful – for better or worse. The momentary idealism of the 2003 American Anti-War movement was bulldozed by the long-running and pre-assembled idealism of Christian Fundementalist xenophobia, American exceptionalism and the Neo Liberal-aided Military Industrial Complex. Bigger ideals trump smaller ideals, just as active beliefs trump ironically reactionary ones.

Perhaps constant irony is the tail end of Post Modernism's relentless deconstruction of all things Modern and prior. In the dust of deconstruction there must be some room made for reasoned faith, convictions beyond the non-stop intellectual negations of Post Modernism and the blind spiritual loyalty of Modernism. Soren Kierkegaard frequently wrote about faith, and believed there to be no other way to gain practical wisdom than to step forward and take risks that would lead to experiencing both success and failure. What if more were willing to believe in something so monumental as progress beyond deconstruction – to enter a world of *belief*, as Bruno Latour describes, "that retain[s] Modernism's feeling of clarity and order, but freed from its ancient connection to hierarchy and verticality"? [5] In a creative environment that prizes articulated ideals instead of the ability to evade criticism, even failure is an honor for those who were willing to have tried to nudge us closer to their utopia.

Written in 2011.

[1] Clay Shirkey, "Here Comes Everybody", 2008. Conference at the Web 2.0 Expo, San Francisco 2008. Online at
http://blip.tv/web2expo/web-2-0-expo-sf-2008-clay-shirky-862384.
[2] Douglas Coupland, *Generation X: Tales for an Accelerated Culture*, St. Martin's Press, New York 1991.
[3] Mark C. Miller, "The Hipness Unto Death: Soren Kierkegaard and David Letterman – Ironic Apologists to Generation X", in *Mars Hill Review*, Issue 7, Winter/Spring 1997. pp. 38 – 52.
[4] *The Merchants of Cool*, PBS Frontline, 2001. Directed by: Barak Goodman. More info: www.pbs.org/wgbh/pages/frontline/shows/cool/.
[5] Bruno Latour, "Some Experiments in Art and Politics", in *e-flux magazine,* Issue 23, March 2011. Online at www.e-flux.com/journal/view/217.

From Clubs to Affinity: The Decentralization of Art on the Internet

Just as society's notion of a single public sphere has transformed into dispersed networks of like-minded affinity, so too has the reception and production of internet art become increasingly decentralized. I will use Jürgen Habermas' 1962 essay *The Structural Transformation of The Public Sphere* as a model to understand what formative shifts have occurred in the past two decades of the internet's existence and the art that has been displayed through it. The first portion of this writing is an attempt to historically situate the internet's role in providing a public sphere for artists. Later, I draw a parallel between post-Y2K social platforms like Facebook and the networked distributional channels many internet artists have been using since the emergence of surf clubs. I conclude with a criticism of art determined by the protocols of the latest networked platforms – such as Tumblr. Instead of a close-read of specific works, I will be focusing on tracing a structural lineage between early examples of canonized internet art, the mid-2000's surf clubs and today's Web 2.0-hosted art communities. By examining their productive and distributive structures, I will provide an understanding of the limitations and freedoms the artists active in these various periods have undergone. It is my hope that by examining these structural pro's and con's internet artists may come to a more ideal conception of future organizational forms.

1. The Creation of Digital Selves

With the release of Netscape Navigator in 1994 and many state-backed projects widening user access, the internet began hosting a massive influx of users eager to explore the new potentials in communication, self-representation and political organization it provided. This cultural phenomenon helped shed the skeptical view many artists previously held toward digital technology – a tendency beginning with the destructive influence cybernetics had in the Vietnam War. In an interview after organizing *Software*, a seminal exhibition of digital and conceptual art at the Jewish Museum in 1970, Jack Burnham explains the difficulties of dealing with the contradictory desires of artists who wanted to make use of digital technology while simultaneously boycotting the corporations producing that digital technology on War-affected moral grounds. In the midst of Vietnam, Burnham goes on to call the future of a digitally focused art "increasingly untenable" [1]. To artists and other cultural producers, the 1990's internet presented an inviting break from the one-to-many distributional structure of corporate newspapers or television. Artists' expectations of the internet's position to share information democratically can be seen as a reinvigoration of the belief in a *public sphere*, described by Jürgen Habermas as a discursive space outside of government or economic influence where individuals are able to communicate freely and come to a common agreement through inclusive participation [2].

Upon its release, the internet seemed capable of combining the positive aspects of previous public spheres into one by mixing the congregational unity of the 19th century English coffee-house or French salon, the decentralized awareness of printed or televised media, and the self-designing agency of local democratic elections. Online existence even managed to provide a key opportunity these previous spaces never could: the ability to create an identity from scratch. Such was the hope of 1990's virtual reality enthusiasts, who designed their online personas through chosen words and graphics. Habermas believed the perversion of previous public spheres was the long-term result of the capitalist economies out of which they arose [3]. Divisions between different sexes, races and classes were widened through market-driven wealth disparities and minority group interests' lack of media representation to the point of creating deep-seated communicational separation. Believers in a virtual utopia hoped to transcend the symptoms of these divisions (such as the perception of difference as seen through living spaces, personal appearance, and spoken dialect, among others) through the digital obfuscation of conditions one was born into and the ability to self-represent oneself through a user-created online avatar. Peter Steiner's 1993 *New Yorker* comic strip joke "On the internet, nobody knows you're a dog" nicely sums up the joyous impossibility of determining who were the digitized voices communicating with each other, rendering the objectively visualized traits necessary for prejudice obsolete.

The 1996 internet art project, "Mouchette" similarly played with the indeterminability of online existence by anonymously producing the sexualized website of a "13 year old girl" complete with the ambiguation of "her" own identity's authenticity. Eva and Franco Mattes' *Darko Maver* (1998) project anonymously created a fictional Serbian artist whose falsified documentation of sculptures were published online and later landed "him" a spot in the Venice Biennale. Multi-user dimensions' (MUDs) and bulletin board systems' (BBSs) participants of that time often presented themselves with mythical handles and graphics, much like the avatar-fueled communities of today's World of Warcraft or Second Life users. As shown by names like JODI.org, Group Z, VNS Matrix, Kasselpunk, ®™ark, 0100101110101101.ORG or YOUNG HAE-CHANG HEAVY INDUSTRIES, prominent internet artists and collectives of that era also veered from traditional identification [4]. The pseudonymity common among 1990's internet users points to their belief in a separation between the fleshly and digital selves they simultaneously inhabited. Virtual reality utopianists did not consider their constructed identity a mask, but a revealing of a 'truer' self stripped of the arbitrary conditions of their inherited existence. As Picasso said, "Art is a lie that brings us nearer to the truth".

After the "Dot Com Bust" and the 9/11 attacks, the internet took on a new social shape, embracing and mandating birth-given identity in America and abroad [5]. This shift towards traditional identification was partly caused by a change in the way digitally invested corporations understood the free labor of internet users as a potentially profitable natural resource. Many post-Y2K businesses shifted away from pay-to-play restricted access and made use of the widespread desire of users to discover, view, and re-circulate information online. Web 2.0 profit was primarily founded on exposure to advertising and data mining the habits of identified users as an informational resource to be sold to marketing firms. Spam was the incompetent and belligerent older sibling of Web 2.0's sophisticated advertising mechanisms – all of which required a return to finding out just *who* was using the internet and *why* they were doing so.

These commercial interests ran parallel with larger governmental efforts to track the lives of named individuals through legislation like America's

Patriot Act, Russia's N 575, or the Great Firewall of China. As German Police and Justice Minister Thomas de Maiziere wrote in his essay *Foundations of a Common Net Policy for the Future*, "The free citizen shows his face, tells his name and has an address." [6] At the dawn of the new millennium, being consensually surveilled was not only the new economic and political duty of law-abiding American citizens, but would soon become a social necessity as well. Recreational internet users of the 1990's emphasis on a multiplicity (or negation) of selves was converted to the heightened construction of one's Facebook profile information, for instance. Web 2.0 social networks like Myspace commanded users to make avatars from their birth-given identities, to self-design their personalities through tagged pictures and comment threads, profiles and quizzes. The online creation of new selves was not over, but this time they would bear the same birth names as their creators or be tagged through university-verified school e-mail addresses. Compared to the previous decade's belief in identity made through imagination, social networks appealed to their user's peer-fostered egos by providing publicly visible friends lists and peer displays of communication to indicate real life popularity. As a result, many users came to believe each event in their lives actually had two authenticating factors: the moment an event occurred in real-time and the moment it was recognized through a digital photograph by a vast audience of peers online. The oft-used net saying "pictures or it didn't happen" isn't just a come-on for proof, but exemplifies Web 2.0's externalization of reality from the eye of the beholder to the informational reciprocation of peers.

2. Art in the Social Network

The 21st century emergence of internet art as a valid artistic form coincided with the rise of Web 2.0 social networks such as Friendster (launched in 2002), Myspace (2003) and Facebook (2004). Preceded by the Walker Art Center's experimental online art space Gallery 9 (1997-2003), in 2003 the new media outlet Rhizome became part of New York's New Museum, effectually canonizing an ongoing institutional position for internet-related art within contemporary art discourse. The mid-2000's defining organizational structure for art online was the surf club. Websites like Nasty Nets, Supercentral and Spirit Surfers were made of 15 to 30 person groups whose members contributed to an ongoing visual-conceptual conversation through the use of digital media. Surf clubs shared some aspects with social networking platforms through continuously occurring posts, communal organization and the performativity of real-time involvement on a publicly visible digital stage. Though born well into the Web 2.0 era, surf clubs took cues from the major social networks of the time while remaining separate institutions from them. The dispersion of art through wholesale involvement within corporately sponsored social networks would not take place for another few years.

Surf club members fulfilled a double role of production and reception by interpreting each other's posts and responding to the previous creator with their own visual art in a chronological display. The club members' conversational insularity within a single space (as delineated by their URL) allowed for a thorough articulation of concepts and aesthetics. Currently prevalent internet art themes such as the readymade-inspired use of default software effects, 'digital shamanism' and the Photoshop manipulated appropriation of vernacular net culture became popularized during this period as a result of the clubs' ability to focus and expand on their fellow members' work. The intended viewership of surf clubs also included non-participating audiences – the URLs could be accessed by non-members as well. In-house surf club trends were highly influential to their external public; many of today's emerging internet artists have claimed the artistic content produced by the clubs' 'legislative bodies' of participants as major influence.

As a literacy-required and internally conversant group made possible by the opening of a vast informational trade border, the history of the surf club shares great similarities with Habermas' conception of the early bourgeois public sphere. Inclusion in a surf club was largely dictated by a prospective member's social affiliations or through a club organizer recognizing another artist's work online [7]. This publicly conversant grouping of communally productive artists separated surf clubs from their forerunners, who had often communicated with each other privately through listservs and displayed projects on individually maintained URLs. Also made apparent by surf clubs was the need for internet artists to produce their own institutional borders to more visibly exist as an art-focused discourse when located on the seemingly infinite plane of online existence – promotional billboards can double as walled barriers and vice versa. The trade off between surf clubs and individual artists' websites was one of openness for efficiency. By creating a meta-organizational structure within the internet, not everyone would be able to participate in posting works, though many more viewers would be able to engage the work of prominent and emerging internet artists during that time due to the convenience of the clubs' unifying site of display.

Habermas describes a similar methodological tension within the early bourgeoisie public sphere: on the one hand, some Renaissance era bourgeoisie wanted to encourage a more broad discussion among a greater percentage of the population while other members wanted to maintain a quality level of opinion-forming discourse without the noise of uninformed masses. This is not to say the early bourgeoisie public sphere advocated a teleological end in its selectivity of members; the public sphere was conceived as an idealized site for ongoing and informed debate free of dogma. Surf clubs also espoused no specified intention beyond serving as a host environment to a series of visual-conceptual jests and responses made by *qualified* members [8]. The surf clubs' initial underdog status soon transitioned to one of institutional success for many members as venues like the Venice Biennale, the New Museum and a slew of international galleries endorsed club participants.

Regarding Habermas's theory, Craig Calhoun states:

> [...] a public sphere adequate to a democratic polity depends upon the quality of discourse and the quantity of participation. Yet the transformations of the public sphere that Habermas describes turns largely on its continual expansion to include more and more participants (as well as on the development of large scale social organizations as mediators of individual participation). [9]

With this in mind, one can see a parallel historical progression of internet artists away from rarified groupings and towards the larger numbers of participants currently using Web 2.0 platforms to publish their work. Habermas considered the mix of unregulated participation and corporatized social organizations (such as newspapers) as the end of a quality debate for the public sphere. Without a space for discourse free of economic pressure, and if public knowledge was controlled by the private interests of printed media, Habermas believed an idealized public sphere would be impossible. However, today's Web 2.0 mass media outlets do not insert informational content for their users, but allow them to distribute self-produced content among one another. Because such a reversal of roles was unanticipated by Habermas, this essay will now draw upon more up to date theories to develop an understanding of contemporary online structures.

Internet art's transition into the dominant social model of its online environment was completed as an emerging group of artists utilized the networked capabilities of Web 2.0 platforms, leaving behind the centralized structure of the surf club and its barriers to membership. Artists new to web-based mediums who lacked social connections to older club members (many of whom had been active since the 90's) found agency in platforms that fully automated the process of blogging and placed the participant in an opportune community of peers united through a shared corporate interface. Tumblr (2007) and Blogger (1999) granted users free hosting, URLs and inner-platform communication options. Feed aggregators like Google Reader (2007) allowed users to simultaneously follow any blog with an RSS feed and receive instant updates on those sites, providing an even more comprehensive opportunity for viewers to keep tabs on the artists of their choosing. Through self-selected aggregation, the Web 2.0 internet art viewer is involved in a relationship of *affinity* to many artists' work as opposed to the contained unity of a surf club. In such a form of peer-to-peer engagement viewers forego the hope to overcome all divisions in taste and resign their interests to ongoing positions of difference. The cohesion of a club becomes unfeasible when each artist and viewer's understanding of 'the internet art world' results from an atomistic, self-tailored exposure through aggregated digital media.

If relations between internet artists using Web 2.0 platforms are best thought of as a form of consensual affinity, the structure of those relations may be understood through Gilles Deleuze's concept of the rhizome, a baseless structure capable of forming links between any two points within it. Deleuze describes the rhizome as a tangle of interconnected nodules working in concert with each other through individual links instead of a common ground. It would be easy to say that all artists work this way and always have – that before the internet an Impressionist painter was influenced by a rhizomatic array of other 19th century painters, for example. But, today's Web 2.0 internet artists are uniquely rhizomatic not based on their source of influence, but because their production of meaning is *externally contingent on a network of other artists' content*. This shift is evidenced in the way Tumblr's practitioners regularly post other artists' work alongside their own without consent. Artists like Brian Khek do not claim creation of the appropriated work they post to their Tumblrs, but contrast the differences in signified content, intention or history between them and others to situate viewers' understanding of their own art. For them, it is important that the viewer interpret the appropriated artist's work as separate from the blogger-artist, or else all meaning generated through juxtaposition would be leveled.

Individuals during and prior to the existence of surf clubs have blogged the work of other artists through Delicious accounts, but to click a Delicious link takes you directly to the website of the artist described. This generation of Web 2.0 artists centralizes others' content around *themselves*, pulling the actual work off of its creator's website and placing it on their own. The difference between past and present linking methods is subtle but telling; linking work on Delicious is a way of saying "I like this", while placing appropriated Tumblr content next to one's own work is a way of saying, in some capacity, "I *am* this". To blog someone else's work is a method of locating disparity and semblance, a gesture that allows artists the ability to situate their interests in a larger field of production while simultaneously announcing themselves as distinct creators. The same can be said of the act of tagging on Facebook or writing on someone else's wall: each is a performative display made to elucidate a connection between separate identities for the spectatorship of an assumed audience. The Web 2.0 artist positions herself as part of an expanding whole – the artist perpetually understood in relation to a self-produced group show. By necessitating the viewership and representation of other artists to define one's self, Web 2.0 artists blur the line between viewing and creating, as each action becomes a continuum of the other.

The context a Web 2.0 artist creates for herself on her Tumblr is not the sole lens through which her work is viewed. She may be subject to appropriation by another artist in her aggregate network – her work now acting as a counterpoint instead of the conceptual anchor. Many websites posting new art exclusively show other artists' work using various logics of info-visualization. A promotional website's organizational voice is determined by its range of content, rate of posting, information included about work, designed display and textual commentary. For most viewers and producers, finding out about a new artist usually results from these well-trafficked promotional blogs, making Web 2.0 artists' context for initial recognition one heavily influenced by the agenda of another website's organizational voice in a process much like gallery or museum representation.

As an artist is included on more organizational blogs the concentric circles of her viewer-perceived image tug increasingly further from their middle point. This rhizomatic pull is even capable of severing the relation of an artist to her own work entirely – each entity living its own existence without many viewers' recognition of who made the work in the first place. Anonymized art usually comes by way of images that have been re-circulated deep within the networks of Web 2.0 users. Just as a tire's treads wear away with use, the contextual backing of an art image is stripped by its own applicability among networked bloggers. In this way, the removal of an artist's name, work title, and date is the highest honor bestowed upon today's networked producer. It is this art that has visually resonated so well its image has preceded its description.

3. Structural Limitations and Peer Influence

Perhaps the most encouraging aspect of Web 2.0 platforms is the decentralization of artistic tendencies, which, instead of being located in only a few places, are displayed through hundreds of individual sites often connected through a blogging service. It would be wrong to assume that determining influence has been removed altogether, though. Network artists would do well to understand the subtle ways art is influenced in lieu of consolidated sites of production, to dissect internet art's chain of aesthetic command (the type of content and form internet artists collectively hold dear, and the visual-conceptual techniques employed by the majority) without the centralized visibility of the surf clubs' guiding influence. The disuse of clubs must be considered alongside a simultaneous rise in constrictions by the protocols of Web 2.0 platforms' structural biases. As Alex Galloway and Eugene Thacker state in "Protocol, Control and Networks",

> protocological control brings into existence a certain contradiction, at once distributing agencies in a complex manner, while at the same time concentrating rigid forms of management and control." [10]

A social economy of reblogged material is an expression of exchange-value. The objective of this system is recurrence – to be bought/reblogged the maximum number of times at the greatest price/digital visibility possible. This process of peer-to-peer dispersion does not mean there is a system of discipline in place for internet artists who step outside the limits of what is artistically 'acceptable', but a series of pre-emptively controlling factors over the type of content circulated within Web 2.0 art networks. This control privileges aesthetic interoperability in a way best articulated through Postel's Law, "be conservative in what you do, be liberal in what you accept from others," which is to say that art produced for Web 2.0 platforms must conservatively anticipate the constrictions of its environment to be most liberally circulated within it. When applied to networks like Tumblr, interoperability should be defined on two levels. First, the formal interoperability of a Web 2.0 work is determined by the categorical distinctions between mediums most blogging services offer. What is not singularly defined as an image, video, or textual piece of content is unable to be transferred through these channels. Web 2.0 users' inability to combine mediums at the moment of production is a severe limitation to the creative process and fosters a regressive, if unintentional, return to medium specificity. Even works that adhere to a single medium are still subject to further scrutiny. For instance, a video artwork that allows users to embed it in a greater number of websites (as opposed to only being viewable through its source, like most Quicktime files) is automatically 'privileged' because it will be able to be appropriated by a wider audience.

As artist Jon Rafman says,

> I think we've reached a point now, in my generation, where we don't even know if we are celebrating something and saying its great and affirming it or if we're engaging in an ironic critique and mocking it. We've almost collapsed the two. [11]

For those unwilling to engage in a critical discourse, this collapse means that visibility is the prime currency of network value, making formal interoperability a factor of utmost importance.

Secondly, the interoperability of content in these networks is greatly determined by the social pressures of rhizomatic production. An artist defining herself in juxtaposition to a peer is only as valuable as their respective projects are meaningfully divergent. What causes this juxtaposition to fail is when network artists make no attempt to specify the point of comparison between their own work and the work of another. This appropriation can be corrupted when artists intend their publishing of another person's work to be an unspoken appeal for reciprocation, especially when that peer can offer greater visibility if she chooses to do so. Artists using platforms like Tumblr should be weary of the addiction originated by those sites' preceding social networks – endless reliance on external validation. Web 2.0's dystopia for recreational and artistic users alike is the loss of a conception of the self in absence of network approval, to believe that we are hollow shells waiting for Facebook comments, Tumblr reblogs, and promotional Tweets to provide the substance of our being. For a generation of internet artists that is admittedly apolitical and tends to bark in the face of intellectualism, a return to medium specificity and aesthetic purity as evinced by the recent embrace of formalist digital 'painting' seems all too fitting.

When artistic value has been subjugated to a mere reliance on visibility, abstract beauty functions as the perfect decor in an arena of political ambivalence. Web 2.0's generation of artists should aspire to creating an art as rich and complex as the environment they inhabit, but it may paradoxically require more of them to stand for something greater than their relations with each other. There is no turning back to previous structures of the internet's public spheres, but for artists perhaps there is a way of combining select aspects from moments in history as a sum greater than its parts.

Try envisioning a world of internet art that embraces the 1990's imaginative negation of birth identity, the surf clubs' considered focus on their peers' work and the decentralized agency of Web 2.0 platforms. That would definitely be an environment worth aspiring to.

2011. Originally published in *491*.

[1] Willoughby Sharp, "Willoughby Sharp Interviews Jack Burnham", in *Arts Magazine*, Vol. 45, No. 2, November 1970, pp. 21-23.
[2] As a military project later taken over by private interests, internet of the 1990s does not live up to an orthodox definition of the public sphere. The California ideology-inspired type of hope I describe is one of use not creation, content not carrier. Eager participants were pleased to use the technology created by other people or companies as a means to their own end, whether social, political or recreational. Beliefs in an end to communicative repression that were founded in technological opportunities previously unavailable must be considered in tandem with the ongoing marketing and product design strategies of the companies responsible for the commercial internet and home computer industries' success. The inclination among these companies has been to promote the perceived autonomy and self-reliance of their buyers when using their products. Everything from the mouse to the desktop to Macintosh's "Rip. Mix. Burn." campaign has attempted to foster users' belief in their own digital agency. For this, the absence of a visible authority governing the internet has been both a reality of use in many situations and a plan constructed to obscure underlying limitations that will be discussed throughout this essay.
[3] Habermas traces a direct link between the simultaneous emergence of a public sphere, democratic governance and capitalism, stating: "It is not possible to demonstrate the existence of a public sphere in its own right separate from the private sphere, in the European society of the High Middle Ages." In Jürgen Habermas, "The Public Sphere", 1973, in Chandra Mukerji, Michael Schudson (Eds.), *Rethinking Popular Culture: Contemporary Perspectives in Cultural Studies*, University of California Press, Berkeley and Los Angeles 1991, p. 399.

[4] Early internet artists so revered the net-specific characteristics of interaction in their digital public sphere that many criticized the work of later internet artists whose work could be viewed offline or without an internet connection as not being true internet art. Such criticism suggests that these pioneers considered the laterally communicative environment of the internet as an integral lens for their work to be viewed through and activated by. While some post-Y2K artists have since came to view this criticism as an elitist mandate, it should be remembered that these early net-specific beliefs were fueled by a belief in egalitarianism – what could be viewed offline could be made private and excluded from the open viewing and participatory domain of the internet's proposed public sphere.

[5] Geert Lovink, "Eva Illouz, Facebook, and the Crisis of The Multiple Self", undated, unpublished, p. 2. Available online at http://goo.gl/1Rp5K.

[6] Ibid.

[7] From a personal interview with Nasty Nets co-founder Marisa Olson on December 13, 2010.

[8] Thomas Beard, "Interview with Guthrie Lonergan", in Rhizome, March 26, 2008, online at http://rhizome.org/editorial/2008/mar/26/interview-with-guthrie-lonergan/.

[9] Craig Calhoun, *Introduction: Habermas and the Public Sphere*, The MIT Press, Cambridge, Massachusetts and London, England. p. 3.

[10] Alex Galloway, Eugene Thacker, "Protocol, Control and Networks", in *Grey Room*, Fall 2004, No. 17, p. 8.

[11] Nicholas O'Brien, "A Conversation with Jon Rafman", in *Bad at Sports*, May 12, 2010, online at http://badatsports.com/2010/a-conversation-with-jon-rafman-nsfw-video/.

Provocative Materiality in the Valley of Death

Art – like water balloons or capitalism – must continually expand in order to serve its purpose. Without room for infinite aesthetic expansion, art risks the possibility of no longer acting as a suitable vehicle for understanding alternative conceptions of reality. Stale and immobile, a frozen conception of acceptable forms or subject matters art may be expressed through would render it incapable of reflecting on anything other than yesterday's concerns by virtue of speaking exclusively through yesterday's artistic language. Steampunks excluded, you can't play an MP3 on a Walkman. For this, the past 100 years of art making have undoubtedly hosted the most rigorous expansion of form and subject matter art has ever seen, carnivorously assuming the previously uncharted territories of performance, digital media, text, archives, identity politics, relational aesthetics, land, body, and many more. At the current moment, the greatest room for expansion appears to be in the field of digital art due to its reliance on rapidly accelerating technology. Digital art expands with each tech invention made, allowing it to piggyback on an endless stream of new potentials in production, social organization and content so long as the minds in Silicon Valley keep thinking and assembly lines in China keep churning.

The same cannot be said for material art, a so-called terminally ill field of art production where the "death of painting" (much like the "death of the author" or, more apocalyptically, "the death of art") is trotted out every other decade in a pitiful cry for attention not unlike a mall goth's feigned attempts at suicide by cutting as lightly as possible into her own skin. It's enough to pretend you're angry with yourself in front of others but never enough to *actually* die. The morbid air accompanying art's stalwart material mediums – sculpture, painting, drawing – is at once a product of the boredom that comes with their old age and the immobilizing possibility that there might not be anything else left to make art from. Today, practically no subject is considered shocking and as for what type of medium art may inhabit almost everything is tolerated – even Pad Thai with your friends in a gallery, for instance. Like a person left sitting for a prolonged time in a bathtub full of their own filth and cold water, these material producers are left with nothing but the paralyzing option to stay still as possible, to on one hand remain true to the colossal weight of their mediums' storied histories or to invariably remix different sections of those histories together in a way that appears to be sacrilege but upon closer inspection is in fact an exercise in devoted fandom. You need to know art history quite well in order to muster the creativity to 'insult' it. Rather than being thought of as bad boys and girls, these historical collage makers share more in common with fan fiction authors who re-animate the ghosts of their favorite TV shows past. What if Dick Van Dyke did a guest appearance on *I Love Lucy*? What if John McCracken collaborated with Amanda Ross-Ho?

Perhaps the associations with death and material art are even more literal than this, though. Obvious are the connections between museum displays of art objects and decaying archaeological artifacts of human existence. Hell, some people actually make art out of embalmed animals and human remains. Pristinely untouchable, the clinical treatment of art objects viewed in institutional space could easily be confused with the silent, orderly procession of a wake, as each family member walks up to the body of their deceased loved one for a solemnly intimate reflection on their lives. Here the object lays in it's final state for all eternity – unless of course it begins to rot of natural causes, in which case there are well-trained departments dedicated to re-touching the faces of art carcasses so to maintain their superficially immortal existence. If life is full of movement and growth, the only time these works of art were ever alive was during their brief tenure in an artist's studio, the one place where they would justifiably be subject to physical alteration. Any change made to an art object after its incubating studio stint would surely be considered necrophilic defilement.

An answer to this Mary Shelley conundrum (how to bring art objects back from the dead) would mean imbuing material art with those characteristics necessary of livelihood. Most important of these characteristics is *movement* and can be thought of in several stages when applied to art objects: movement-before-exhibition, movement-during-exhibition, and movement-after-exhibition. Movement changes the art object's status from being a purely visual aid into becoming a disembodied relic of the artist's agency, 'performing' in the real world as a material satellite of intention while never fully committing to a single status; movement infers ongoing transformation.

This perpetual state of becoming is at odds with traditional notions of art objects that seek to create fixed, iconic structures and visuals. In the infinitely moving art object we find the potential for the work to maintain constant relevance through time, to shift alongside art itself in its ongoing expansion of form. This isn't an attempt to bring dead objects back from the grave but a thought about how to make an art incapable of death itself. The secret of moving art objects' longevity is that they introduce the agency of more people than just the originating artist, opening a Pandora's Box of different amendments that could potentially be made to a work. If one person can influence the becoming of an art object, why not all? And why not to the greatest degree possible? The moving art object would ideally not be recognizable to itself a brief time after it was first made.

Movement-before-exhibition is a concept most people are already familiar with, as it is a conceptual device often used in process-based art. Here the art object, in its physical state, exists in equal importance with the history of its being. Movement-before-exhibition is a way of valuing conceptual provenance – the resume of a given thing's past as it has traveled through cultures, time, processes, or various forms of ownership. The object moved before exhibition is supposed to act as an artifact of its own existence; it is both the thing that moved and the documentation of that very movement. Movement-before-exhibition is the least lively of the three types because the moment of exhibition is when and where these objects cease moving, becoming a statue of their once lively existence.

Movement-during-exhibition can be thought of as art that is participatory, where over the course of the exhibition objects are added to, subtracted from, or otherwise altered. Here the value of the object is produced through the way its viewership contributes to and interacts with it. The use, relations, or affect participants experience during their alteration of this art provides the conceptual focus of the project. Finally, movement-after-exhibition has historical precedent in the tradition of mail art, a medium where the moment of exhibition for each object exists during the brief time span when a recipient owns the mailed object before shipping it off yet again to another person. It is inferred the object will be in continuous motion, periodically resting between an infinite number of trips.

One factor inhibiting the movement of all three stages is the convention that each of these types of art objects be characterized as art throughout the process of their creation. When art is in past, present or future movement it rarely escapes its own shadow as a work of art – effectively eliminating a wide range of other movements and interactions it could be granted if it were to exist as an everyday object. The pretext of what is being shipped as 'art' affords it a kind of preciousness not experienced by other goods that are rapidly consumed, traded, or destroyed according to their utility or signified worth. In movement-before-exhibition the object is likely kept under the watchful eye of the directing artist, who coordinates pre-planned changes. Movement-during-exhibition means that viewer participation occurs under the surveillance of the gallery or museum – places with such rigid histories of enforced viewer docility that guards often keep a watchful eye on those wild enough to desire to take a photograph to send to their relatives. It's telling that Ray Johnson (like fellow social sculptor Joseph Beuys) maintained a series of trademark stamps and small drawings to differentiate his movement-after-exhibition mail art from normal types of mail. These stamps acted as a way of alerting future participants that the thing they were encountering was in fact art and to treat it as such. This convention of contextualization seems to contradict the spontaneity that makes moved art objects so exciting. The idea of movement infers an escape from the author's grasp and leap (if only temporary) into the unknown, into the everyday. Is it possible that we have babysat art objects to death? What if their re-invigoration will require us to set them free, to let them stay out late past their locational curfew? If so, there is yet another type of movement as worthy as the three previously mentioned; it is the idea of *contextual* movement.

Art projects that rely on contextual movement are perceptual shape shifters, changing on the basis of their different audiences' understanding of them. These shifts in perception necessarily produce a range of diverse reactions; the subtle differences in subjectivity that allow for a group of people to understand a given thing as entertainment, pornography, art, or blasphemy are capable of producing discourses far more complex than those of an object perceived as a work of art alone. To harness and display these divergent interests requires, at first, a kind of decontextualization. If institutions pre-empt the status of objects as art, we should look to those sites without single purposes for the objects they house as potentially liberating domains for the placement or incubation of context-moving art: the streets, unsuspecting homes, stores, the internet, outer space, etc. Here the responsibility of the artist is both a discrete creator and silent archivist, documenting alterations to or interactions with her perceptually slippery work as it 'lives' [1]. It is necessary to maintain some anonymity (or pseudonymity, the job of assuming a separately false guise from your given name) throughout the process of contextually moving art, or else the format of pronounced authorship risks outing itself as being separate in some way from every other object that exists without a personalized 'made by' stamp.

At the intersection of these notions of objecthood, movement, and anonymity exists a website that trades in all three. Silk Road was created in February 2011 as an anonymous online marketplace. Users are only able to access the website through the anonymizing browser software Tor and are only able to buy goods by trading in the anonymous digital currency Bitcoin. After signing up, users are given viewing access to an inventory of objects, services, and information for sale, though most of what comprises Silk Road's marketplace are illegal drugs. While the internet brazenly traffics in the dispersion of outlawed kinds of information, the movement of humans and objects remains determined by governmental law. What is most interesting about the Silk Road is its ability to use the internet to blur those lines between national dictates, effectively establishing an agorismic realm outside their control. Here the idea of movement and objecthood takes on an altogether different character as the boundaries of personal liberty as regulated through law are considered instead of this writing's previous subject of art's aesthetic boundaries. But are they so different? At what point may the law itself become a subject of artistic involvement, not in the sense of a depictive or figurative response, but direct movement *in and through it*? Here materiality finds yet another source of life, as the implications of objects that are legally disputed may, unto themselves, serve as catalysts for the most dire of punishments. Being dead is a pretty safe bet, being alive is much riskier. On the Silk Road are objects that *people move* between each other while those objects simultaneously *move people*, scrambling states of consciousness, forming black market economies of employment, and potentially landing some in jail. There is an energy emitted from this contraband that no plaster mold or stretched canvas could ever project – the possibility of *real risk*, as opposed to the simulated risk of offending art history.

There is much overlap between material art that relies on contextual movement and art objects that use the law as their medium. This is because many objects that are illegal in one country may not be in the next; the law varies from place to place. Thinking of contraband as an inherently conflictive form of materiality draws to mind Claire Bishop's writing on the subject of relational antagonism, an idea she proposed in response to Nicolas Bourriaud's largely utopian description of Relational Aesthetics. In her essay *Antagonism and Relational Aesthetics* [2] Bishop theorized a type of relational art that, instead of promoting peaceful harmony between participants, uses a social space to reveal the underlying tensions or civil inequities of a community. Contraband is comprised of a kind of relationally antagonistic materiality, it is a physical footnote of disputed ethics, morals, economic and political agendas capable of quickly exposing or igniting those beliefs wherever it goes. The simple existence of contraband is enough to enact a long chain of relational events; just consider the word *possession* in this art and illegal object dichotomy.

Of course contextually moving work and the use of contraband are only two ways of expanding the domain of material art production. They are possible solutions to a problem shockingly few are willing to admit: material art making is no longer at the edge of the avant-garde, it has become a decorative field of production seeking to find the limits of buyers' and curators' tolerance for purchase and exhibition inclusion rather than defining the philosophically murky edges of what art is. Most morose is the inclination to believe that nothing new is possible for art, that post-modernity has subordinated makers to a position of permanently being formal and historical DJs, remixing a slew of endlessly forgettable artworks-cum-mixtapes. We've wallowed in the death of originality, art, the author and everything else for long enough. Let's at least try to do something new and alive – art objects may currently be dead, but we aren't.

[1] Alternately, there is the option of releasing what was an art object in to the wild without recouping its existence. In this scenario the contexts the object was viewed through would inevitably shift as well but not be made available to later viewers, meaning the project would assume a performative, rather than process-based or sculptural purpose. This is the difference between wildlife keepers who release animals in the wild and others who keep GPS trackers on them.

[2] Claire Bishop, "Antagonism and Relational Aesthetics", in *October 110*, Fall 2004, pp. 51 – 79.

The Many Faces of Tumblr

Out of the millions of Tumblrs in existence, the type I'm most interested in are the ones R. Gerald Nelson describes in his text *DDDDoomed* [1] – the image aggregators (henceforth abbreviated as 'IAs') whose creators rapidly compile image after image of the cultural artifacts surrounding them, stripping their visuals of any contextual backing. Nelson begins his talk of IA's by comparing those authors who "[present] disparate images as a way of portraying the idiosyncrasies of our culture(s)" against those who "narcissistically and merely [attempt] to communicate one's keen eye for style and trends." The most egregious offense of the second, narcissistically-inclined IA, Nelson says, is when they consider their text-free posts of Nan Goldin photographs next to images of Urban Outfitters scarves to be *art*. I am nowhere near as zealous as Nelson on this distinction, as my own experiences have led me to believe most anything can be considered art (though that doesn't imply most anything can be considered *good* art). Things that are temporarily considered art can simultaneously serve other non-art functions. Yes, in literal terms Tracey Emin's installation *My Bed* can be jumped on or slept in but this idea can also be interpreted in an even broader sense – sometimes making art can serve as a great way to get laid, or get a job teaching, or meet new friends.

In this case, I believe IAs to be an instrument of brand making; visual culture used as an interpersonal lubricant and method of heightening self-awareness. Conversely, IA's are also the product of the hipster culture industry and the advertising world's wet dream, but I'll get to all of that.

The first function IAs serve is to bring their users one step closer to completing their identities' digital existence. In the transition from a physical to a digital social life, Web 2.0 users make use of whatever number of platforms they think necessary to sculpt the limbs of the digital bodies. It is the objective of companies like Facebook or Google to become the sole platform necessary for online interaction, creating what are known as walled gardens for their users. At the present moment, our digital bodies still lust for greater articulation, for a wider array of outlets than a single platform to express our knowledge and personalities. Although Twitter and Facebook's status update features are nearly identical in appearance, they each boast high volumes of participation because the two sites are able to maintain separate social atmospheres for communication, allowing their users more opportunities to diversely articulate themselves. The average IA user sees the communicative opportunities of Tumblr as a chance to show a different side of her self not possible through other platforms.

Every anonymous image posted to an IA is at best a marker of visual awareness, enacting a psychic game of recognition between online peers. An image is not just a proclamation of affinity, but a link back to that person's browsing habits, a way of selectively revealing one's own net history. Like a group of friends struggling to prove they know the lyrics of their favorite songs in front of each other as they sing next to a radio, group consciousness of a decontextualized image's history serves as a social unifier. Those who are satisfied to circulate such images without an awareness of their signified content are the least productive Tumblr users because their actions do not help clarify or proclaim any aspect of their cultural knowledge. Mindless reblogging will likely obscure a person's true nature to her viewers by associating her with a visual message she would otherwise not consent to if she were more fully aware of its implications. This tendency of poor self design is similar to if a Facebook user were to copy and paste a status update of her friend's that was written in Russian because the unintelligible letters "looked nice together".

I'm being hard on naïve Tumblr users, but the truth is that even the most naïve use of Tumblr is more productive than the television-viewing alternative. As Clay Shirky says of the supposedly lowly middle age men pretending to be elves on World of Warcraft, "at least they're doing something... It's better to do something than to do nothing." [2] Naïve users of Tumblr are a promising example of that platform's egalitarian acceptance of all – without them, the platform would be restricted to only those with the necessary pedigree to do "proper blogging". As Ted Nelson said in *Dream Machines*, "We are all naïve users at some time or other; it's nothing to be ashamed of. Though some computer people tend to think it is." [3]

When compared to the two hundred billion hours a year Americans alone spend watching televised programs often designed to numb their critical capacity and reduce their minds to commercially consumptive husks, searching and selecting from a vast sea of images – even if only with the hopes of finding what one deems cool-looking – is a more productive media activity for raising one's level of aesthetic self consciousness than having those images chosen for you. There is a certain cultural athleticism often required to have a popular Tumblr, an innate ability to find not just the most obscure, tasteful versions of a single subject matter but to coast across a variety of subject matters and to post those findings at a regular rate. For this reason, posting images of art next to fashion next to web ephemera is not an idiosyncrasy on the part of the IA's poster, but a gesture meant to show one's prowess in disparate cultural fields. However, this belief in Tumblr as a productive refiner of taste may only be true to the extent that one believes Tumblr is not just a more *sophisticated* commercial advertising mechanism than television – which could also very well be the case. What is productive about an IA's constant shuffling of images could simultaneously be a user-generated advertising campaign in disguise – two realities present at once depending on how an IA is interpreted.

For people posting images on an IA, being a physical owner of the objects visualized or a true actor of lifestyles visually depicted is of no concern to others. You don't need to *own* the shoes you posted to your Tumblr so long as you *know* about those shoes. You don't need to *go* to the concert so long as you *know* where the Mediafire file is. There is undoubtedly a longing for the material culture of the past spoken through today's IAs' digitally communicative methods. We're not over objects – it's just more efficient to identify with them in absence of their bulky presence. In a Baudrillardian sense, image awareness of culture has been equated with cultural participation itself – one's brand depicted on Tumblr is inseparable from her true physical being.

Because most every user of Tumblr is in all likelihood also a viewer of other people's Tumblrs, each user is subjected to a wide array of new artworks, pieces of clothing, lifestyles and more. This viewing process is capable of creating known un(kn)owneds for a viewer, triggering research into new ideas to possibly reblog on one's own Tumblr or associate with in (gasp) real life. Most of this is a process of cultural calibration – fine tuning what kinds of GPOYs are acceptable, learning different flavors of irony through catch phrases and memes – though these digital encounters inevitably have real life implications on the food we eat, the clothes we buy, the (old) media we spend time viewing, the bars we go to and most other every day experiences. To become a visual scholar on Tumblr and not think it would have an effect on all of the visually concentrated products and experiences we pay for would be far from the truth.

I often wonder if the great number of products circulated on Tumblr is not an ad-man's dream? The advertising industry has had an uphill battle for a while now because the second an average consumer recognizes she is being convinced to buy a product she instantly becomes skeptical of that item's worth due to the profit incentives of the seller. With IAs, you have peers advertising clothing, drugs, food and more to *each other*. This isn't a come-on to try a product from The Man, this is a hot tip from your stylish friends! It's fitting that no specific product has benefitted significantly more than others due to viral marketing on Tumblr – that singular, stalwart support for any one thing would be an anathema of the way IAs work to constantly refresh themselves. Instead, Tumblr has supported the wide-ranging hipster culture industry (or, lifestyle) in general more than any one particular thing. This may be because the hipster culture industry is most perfectly represented through the standards of proper IA use; a feverish search for the new proposed as a self-aware indexing of the forgotten past. Nowhere can you be a hipster quite as efficiently as you can online. Time simply moves too slow in real life for that. On Tumblr you can propose hundreds of new outfit variations, though in an AFK trip to the bar you can probably only wear one outfit per evening – what a drag. Real life demands that you go to sleep at some point and put down your art history book, though on Tumblr you are able to place your posting settings on for every 5 minutes so you can stream hundreds of new art images overnight.

For this, I love Tumblr because it allows us to be a little more than human – an effect quite opposite of most digital life. In the tradition of the avant-garde's desire to collapse boundaries between art and every day life, I see Tumblr as a remarkable tool. More importantly than collapsing distinctions, IAs are a way to *create* unforeseen connections between disparate cultural poles. With IAs we have a chance to gain a greater art-informed appreciation for worthy cultural relics long deemed non-art and perhaps a chance to forget about the endless garbage heaps of forgettable art only present in our discourse because it has been contextualized as such.

My only hope, in digging through the visual crates of the past and spreading it among each other like wild fire, is that we don't forget to create our own art indicative of contemporary life. How odd it would be, if in 50 years the internet archaelogists assigned to dig up 2011's time capsule discovered we consisted of nothing but the time capsules of those before us.

Written in 2010.

[1] R. Gerald Nelson, *DDDDoomed – Or, Collectors & Curators of the Image: A Brief Future History of the Image Aggregator*, Edition MK, 2010.
[2] Clay Shirky, "Gin, Television, and Social Surplus", in *Worldchanging, Ma*y 7, 2008. Online at www.worldchanging.com/archives/008009.html.
[3] Ted Nelson, *Computer Lib/Dream Machine,* Self-published, 1974, revised 1987.

Making The Best of a Permanent Pay Freeze

It's hard to believe that, for as many people as there are currently looking for a job, there was a time in the early 1970's when Americans were revolting against work. The slogan "Jobs for life" was, at the time, seen as a life sentence to office conformity or repetitive factory tasks. Andrew Ross says in his book *Nice Work If You Can Get It: Life and Labor in Precarious Times* that there was a "visceral protest against the long-term tedium of organizational employment," resulting in "sabotage, chronic absenteeism, and wildcat strikes." [1] Around this time (prior to the massive industrial outsourcing that would later occur) many American union members were beginning to feel as though their organizational employment was tokenistic, viewing their laborer status as a fixed position that allowed for little say in larger managerial matters. As a perverted response to this air of alienation, "flexible work" and self-employment were frequently offered and imposed by corporate management on workers in the decades to come. Workers took these jobs on in droves because, as Ross says, "neoliberalism ... exploits the credo that individuals have power over their economic destinies." [2] Since then, many policymakers have come to laud the artist as the new model worker for being self directed, entrepreneurial, accustomed to precarious, non-standard employment, and attuned to producing career hits [3]. For Britain especially, the stereotype of the starving artist has now been transformed into a risk-taking capitalist adventurer of the New Economy. What an odd turn of events.

After factory outsourcing and the dot-com bust, national and local governments worldwide looked to infuse their urban economies by stimulating the entrepreneurial energies of activities now grouped together as the "creative industries," a loose term used to describe artists, entertainers, and architects, as well as the knowledge work of lawyers and financiers [4]. If this term sounds familiar, it's likely because it's the grandchild of the Frankfurt School's Marxist description of the 'culture industry'. However, when Tony Blair's Department of Culture, Media and Sports described the newly dubbed creative industries in their founding documents, the term was molded to express all of the New Economy's signature points of emphasis: technological enthusiasm, the cult of youth, branding and monetization fever, and ceaseless organizational change [5]. Furthermore, in the landscape of cultural production, there was at that time, and continues to be, a huge rush in self-publication and amateur content promotion through websites like YouTube, Flickr, Twitter, Friendster, Second Life, Facebook, and Myspace. Bureaucrats and gatekeepers be damned; fostering the creativity of the young, hustling masses became a top priority of urban policymaking. As such, there seems to be no single group of people more indicative of the new creative industries than contemporary internet artists – the zenith of techno-enthused youth, precarious employment, and do-it-yourself vigor.

While the ethics of artists' compensation have long been a disputed matter, arguably no group of artists has garnered such large, global audiences while so successfully evading payment as those who exist online today. Among the options pursued to sell this art, some have offered property contracts for collectors to buy artist's websites. These contracts are ultimately rental agreements with ICANN, not fully realized ownership in the sense a physical painting provides. Additionally, digital files sold on thumb drives that were ever posted online have likely been saved to someone else's desktop and are able to be endlessly passed on for everyone else to own without any collector's say in the matter. At the root of internet art's unsellability is the point that internet art (like all digital data) is infinitely reproducible, making any attempt to harness it for sale an exercise in maintaining artificial scarcity. Adding to this square peg in a circular hole dilemma is the way in which the cultural rationale of digital content's merit is at opposite ends with that of traditional property valuation; the digital world values content according to its ubiquity (memes, traffic statistics) while the physical world values the scarcity of goods (lower supplies equal higher demands). There isn't nearly enough money in AdSense for individual artists to make a living from advertisements, and it is unlikely any marketing firm will pay for viewer statistics from a single artist's website any time soon. The only other avenue digital content industries have pursued to make money from their creative output has been to control the distribution of works by enforcing copyright law punishments on individuals guilty of recirculating intellectual property without authorization. This method would likely not be supported because most internet artists actually rely on the appropriation of their images through aggregating blogs to make a name for themselves. The precarity of internet-based art production is now only partially remedied when artists venture into traditional economies based on the attention they've been able to attract online. Popular solutions include creating internet-inspired physical objects for gallery sale, knowledge work in academia, or using software skills commercially. Again, nice work if you can get it, but only a lunatic would enter an intentionally restrictive luxury economy with hopes of instantly finding stable employment when there are 90,000 students a year graduating with bachelors degrees in fine art from America alone.

So, if precarity is not going away any time soon for (internet) artists, how can this payless situation be made as culturally generative as possible? Even if it is deserved, not all things must be done for money, and the utopian under-pinnings of art may be a perfect example of something that provides great rewards even when done without pay. In addition to the lure of financial self-achievement, Ross considers the creative industries appealing to people because they promise "the mental challenges and sensuous self-immersion [that are] associated with a surfeit of pleasure and satisfaction." [6] The word 'sustainability' comes to mind when considering a payless activity. If internet art is not a viable career, how can it be made a sustainable cultural ecosystem for those willing to pursue it precariously? Ecologies are successful when actors express themselves and come to common understandings of purpose, boundaries of involvement, and mechanisms for punishment and reward to insure progress. Internet art's current platforms for validation use likeability and shareability as their metrics of success. This is a positive development in art's history insomuch as it is populist and takes in the opinion of many more than we are accustomed to when judging culture, but we may be throwing the baby out with the bath water in the process. Our eyes and attention spans are frivolous things; they move according to our lowest common denominator of desires – has anyone seen how many views a topless photo on Flickr receives? Likes and reblogs are the social currency of what Malcolm Gladwell calls a culture of *weak ties*, where participants have low barriers to entry and correspondingly low returns on their cultural sustainability. Gladwell believes the digital generation's weak ties are a result of how little sacrifice is required of participants to be considered part of any socially networked cause. Others have described this digital façade of risk-free consensus as slacktivism. In short, social networks are able to mobilize the appearance of large quantities of people, but the quality of those group's intentions suffer due to low investments of time, effort, and risk.

Opposite of populism, art's institutional bureaucracy has strong (if conflicting) conceptions of quality but regulates those ideas at the limiting expense of the majority of participating artists and viewers. With 80% of American museum revenues coming from wealthy private sources, it's easy to see how unmarketable art could be forgotten and forgettable art could be marketed in its place, meaning the art institutionally described as influential may be less valuable to other artists or the public than it is important to specific collectors. Between these polemics, there must be a way of acknowledging what is "good" in art without resorting to the equally shortsighted visions of elitism or mob rule. An alternate means for judging art requires no less than a dreadedly *objective* criterion. One idea populists and connoisseurs alike may agree upon is the notion that *good art influences many people*. Here traditional art historians' project of providing a lineage for artists is combined with the populists' goal of uniting the greatest number of people around a common theme. In the phrase *good art influences many people*, what is *good* is interiorly defined according to what is *influential*, an adjective significantly less contentious than wading through the infinite number of definitions for a word like *quality*. This is to say internet art's economy of attention should be re-formulated around a culture of *influence*, and most importantly, continued peer revision. Originators should not be applauded as being "right" for being first but for initiating ongoing conversations, be they visual or otherwise.

The attention economy is an evolutionary remnant of one-to-many media relations past, a fossil from the days when viewership was synonymous with passivity. How many views did the televised Super Bowl get? How many subscribers does the *New York Times* have? These viewership statistics are ways of gauging an audience that has no input in the culture they consume; their attention is monitored because that is all they can contribute. An environment of active cultural participants online looks forward to sustained *dialogue* as a marker of resonance. The blogging and communication platforms currently in use must be remade in the image of articulated response, collaboration, versioning, and displayed influence to sustain meaningful rewards for those brave or foolish enough to take the precarious risk of internet art making. To do so requires no less than the invention of new systems for art's validation online; the medium is still the message. "Likes" and "reblogs" are beginning to feel like tokenistic examples of support. We should create online organizations that foster something more substantial for one another.

2011. Originally published in *Dis Magazine*.

[1] Andrew Ross, *Nice Work If You Can Get It: Life and Labor in Precarious Times*, NYU Press, New York 2009, p. 5.
[2] Ibid., p. 6.
[3] Ibid., p. 7.
[4] Ibid., p. 17.
[5] Ibid., p. 19.
[6] Ibid., p. 18.

The Emergence of Dual Sites

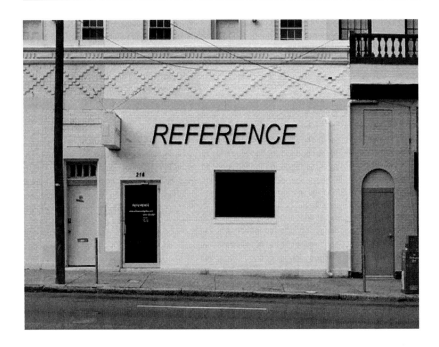

Long ago, artists outsourced the ability to define themselves by granting that right to private media, galleries and museums. In doing so, a major gulf formed between artists who identified with the work claiming to represent their time and those who found little resonance in an art so closely entwined with profit motivations. In asking, "What museum represents me?" or even "What publicly known artists have the same interests as me?" many found the answer was non-existent. In the lives of young artists, the internet is a place to find one's self through the existence of others – to individually reclaim the ability to self-mythologize and empathetically pick from your peers for influence. Thus, internet art is marked by the compulsive urge of searching (or, surfing) to connect with others in a way that is not directed by private interests, but found and shared among individuals. The Dual Site is an institution born from this individuated system of relating with one another. It is an exhibition space symptomatic of physical and digital commingling – an example of how art, like life itself, now exists somewhere between the two.

Dual Sites* are not galleries as we have traditionally known them. As the Future Gallery's director Mike Ruiz states, selling art "is by no means the goal nor motivation for running our space." Perhaps this fact, more than any other, separates the Dual Sites from their predecessors: they seek to create social capital for artists in lieu of money, not because of (or for) pay.

Instead of manipulating their space in a way that would allow them to satisfy the potentially more profitable demand of others, Dual Sites' directors have compartmentalized their efforts as a satisfaction of the *self*. Just who these selves are is precisely what makes this new breed interesting. These gallery directors are like the rest of us; the highly attuned online art viewership who opens every link possible, whose self-spun perception of contemporary work is a web of young, ambitious and gallery-unrepresented peers. The insider status of directors is evidenced in the young artists popularized on the internet who are shown by these spaces.

With such accessibility in mind, it should come as no surprise that Mexico City's Preteen Gallery co-exists as a home for its directors while other Dual Sites, like Richmond Virginia's Reference Art Gallery, are thrifty commercial spaces rented out. Zurich's Paloma Presents doesn't even have a permanent space and migrates from city to city, occupying other galleries in Milan, Lausanne, Basel and more. By making the barrier to entry of opening a Dual Site the possession of a living room and an internet connection, these galleries leave the bureaucracy accompanying the immense funding required of commercial projects out in the wind. Of course, anyone can *start* a gallery this way, but it takes real effort for these spaces to generate viewers' trust through continual maintenance and consistent taste in the artists shown.

Some readers will be quick to associate Dual Sites as an extension of Chicago's rich history of alternative art spaces operating in the face of geographic rejection or the Salon de Refuses endorsement of artists institutionally deemed unworthy. These historical connections are accurate, but we must not ignore what is one of the Dual Sites' most engaging traits: their ability to exist anywhere and to show the work of willing artists from anywhere. So decentralized are their locations, foot traffic is supplementary to the online viewership these galleries command. Jericho Ditch, a Dual Site in Pope Swamp, Virginia, proudly boasts that it has almost no formally art educated gallery goers in person. Invigorating local art communities with access to contemporary work is an intention many Dual Sites share, though their larger function resides with the majority of their viewership online.

Our appreciation of a resume is largely made up of recognizing accomplishments that we did not attend. Facebook invitations to Dual Sites' shows are a telling part of their existence. Most of those invited to attend are not actually asked to visit, but to recognize the existence of an event – to believe it took place, and in doing so, value the exemplified support for the artists shown. Attendance can take place by viewing (or re-blogging) installation images, reading the exhibition essay or logging on to the live cam during the show's opening. It may strike some as odd that a group of artists who exist and organize digitally still rely on physical presentation for communal validation, but I believe the Dual Site's physicality is merely a stand in for viewership's appreciation of something else: dedicated labor and consideration towards the work shown.

To appreciate what a Dual Site offers requires an understanding of what its primary alternative, the image dump Tumblr, is. The endorsement of an artist on Tumblr is a contradiction because the point of the page is to flush itself out of old content as quickly as possible, to move on to new material in hopes of piquing a wider range of viewers through a wider range of content. This makes for a supremely effective source of mass image dissemination, but not one that privileges individual efforts or, necessarily, authorship. Artists often seek the permanence of inclusion on a website that archives its participants and the proper contextualization that a well-written introductory essay provides. The attention garnered from being the front page of a Dual Site's homepage for even two weeks dwarfs the five minutes an artist may have before being replaced by another re-blog on a Tumblr. The effort that goes into creating the physical space and installing exhibits reveals the Dual Site as a provider of considered, though occasional, events as opposed to Tumblr's care free and constant stream. The Dual Site offers what Tumblr is designed not to grant through the effort necessitated by its endorsement – physicality is just a means to this end. Effort is a currency of conviction; a way of validating belief that the work presented is worth the precious digital and physical time given to it.

The emergence of Dual Sites is a milestone for art on the internet because it signifies the supply of an audience so dedicated that their viewing demands are worth being satisfied by the creation of new institutions. Without successfully finding the existence of an online community eager to see its participants awarded for their art, the efforts of Dual Sites would likely go un-attempted, as the social capital awarded by them is only as valuable as the number of people able to recognize it. Instead, the anarchic and altruistic qualities of art's presentation online have been met with a mode of accreditation equally promising.

Written in 2010.

* Extra Extra, The Future Gallery, Gambia Castle, Jericho Ditch, New Jerseyy, Nudashank, Paloma Presents, Preteen Gallery, Reference Art Gallery, Scott Projects.

New Productive Systems

"Technology will in the near and farther future increasingly turn from problems of intensity, substance, and energy, to problems of structure, organization, information, and control."
- Jon von Neumann, member of the Manhattan Project and inventor of the first useful computer, 1949

Introduction

The 'new' in art is often said to be a product of its creators' historical zeitgeist. For instance, the Dadaist's propensity for the irrational is explained as a result of the way World War I's unprecedented mechanical violence shattered the dream of a seemingly inevitable industrial utopia. Or how when historians mention the academicism of the founding conceptual fathers, it is frequently raised in light of their being the first generation of artists that were predominantly university educated. Even the consumption-focused art of Jeff Koons, Sherrie Levine, and Barbara Kruger is couched in reaction to the 1980's neo-liberal policies of economic expansion and corporate wealth. So, while in retrospect it may not be very revelatory to say "art is a sign of the times," there is nothing that draws ire more than for a writer to suggest which cultural events are guiding the generational moment of her existence, or to typify how art has been produced in relation to those events. Perhaps this is because those who do not make art relevant to such typifications tend to believe their importance is threatened by exclusion. Understandably, every living artist shares a stake in recognizing what is contemporary, making it both an accessible and contentious subject matter.

Of the range of things that may be considered new in art today, the tendency among artists to organize internet-based systems for the production of art by other participants – henceforth described as *productive systems* – holds particular salience. Because of these systems' resistance to traditional methods of art analysis, I will offer new criteria for critically understanding them. Just as the historical avant-garde used the latest technologies to expand the field of what may be considered art, what is novel about these productive systems is influenced by Web 2.0's network construction of value and the ability to produce one's own utopian 'space' online.

There is something valuable, if inherently flawed, about artists working toward a definition of what makes themselves and their peers different from their predecessors at the moment of their being. "You weren't there" is the most damning criticism one can launch at a historian, and for good reason. Not only does the historian's absence remove her from the subtle intricacies of the moment she studies but it also forces her to subjectively assign importance to whatever amount of first hand evidence she is able to gather. It has been said that art that is given a description is dead by the time those words reach the air, but nothing is as morbid as pure silence. Those who believe the saying "what can't be found on the internet does not exist," must be amazed at their capability to articulate all that is still unexplained online. This essay is an attempt to provide a generative description for one such phenomenon.

1. The Hive, Bees and Honey

This first section is an attempt to establish a theoretical framework for understanding the multi-faceted nature of productive systems. Some of the artists this essay describes are facilitators for various systems of art's production on the internet. This is to say that they deal in the so-called aesthetics of administration; the invention of a participatory matrix through which others may assert relations and display visual-conceptual content of their own. Productive systems dynamically accrue meaning from the ongoing interventions of their participants through time. This interactivity requires a four-dimensional mode of interpretation. Critics and viewers should recognize productive systems as sites permanently in progress. As a system's content is modified, the discourse surrounding it must be as well, in order to remain applicable. While it is possible to look back and single out a productive system's governing interface, individual relations between users, or specific content displayed through it, none of these individual examples may be used to explain the system as a whole and thus should be seen as merely partial, if helpful, characterizations when reflected on separately. A journalistic blogging approach to criticism may be best suited to address specific elements of these projects as they unfold. Through a writing format that is continuously adaptable, the critic preemptively acknowledges the fleeting nature of her subject matter. Alternately, critics may reflect on a productive system using a narrative approach, identifying the broad-sweeping changes in user contributions leading up to its current state.

Temporal criticism should be applied to each of the various sources of aesthetic merit that comprise a productive system. These conceptually separate (though functionally related) traits may be thought of as the difference between a hive, its bees, and the honey they produce. Previous analytic methods in art have largely offered criticism on the basis of formalist standards or conceptual intention relative to signifiers contained in the 'honey' aspect of this metaphor – the completed visual art products that fill history books and museums. Such analytic methods will not be sufficient to approach what is valuable about the existence of a 'hive' or 'bees' as art in regards to today's productive systems. Instead, I propose an assessment of these systems based on a new, three-pronged set of criteria:

a. the aesthetics of interfacial architecture

b. the quality of Relational value among participants

c. the commonality of visual content produced

Each of these criteria simultaneously offers a void to be filled and an embedded proclamation for developing a new language for the objects of their criticism. Respectively, the proclamations embedded in these criteria read:

a. The interfacial architecture of a system that facilitates digital interactions compels not only a social and political dimension, but allows for the consideration of an aesthetic one as well.

This proclamation runs contrary to the notion that technology is utterly determined by the societal or economic context in which it's created. While these contexts are certainly influential on technology coming to be, so too may technology exert its influence on its human inventors, as was obviously the case with the re-organization of society due to the printing press, radio, television and so on. There is an ebb and flow relationship between humans and technology, as each one simultaneously guides the fate of the other. Providing a more polemic example of this notion of reversed influence and the perpetual interplay of human will in the face of technological opportunity and limitation, environmentalist Denis Hayes concludes:

> **The increased deployment of nuclear power facilities must lead society toward authoritarianism. Indeed, safe reliance upon nuclear power as the principal source of energy may only be possible in a totalitarian state. [1]**

In other words, as the theorist Langdon Winner states:

> **the adoption of a given technical system actually requires the creation and maintenance of a particular set of social conditions as the environment of that system. [2]**

If it is feasible to conceive of technology as producing an authoritarian or egalitarian disposition for those in its presence, so too is it within reason to believe the function of technology also presents its own ethical and aesthetic concerns. In the case of productive systems, the criteria I seek to establish is one of aesthetic judgment for what conditions are necessitated by the use of their interfaces and also how such a system's existence relates to or is situated within the wider fields of art history and social media. There is simply no such thing as a 'neutral' or 'natural' structure for art to exist through, whether this is via a museum, a Tumblr, or one of the systems applicable to this writing.

Design's purpose is often to obfuscate the intention of whatever its underlying mechanism may be. By decoding the architecture of a productive system, a critic may locate the facilitator's concealed ideology for bringing such a project into existence. This first proclamation could be read as an attempt to apply the analytic methods of Institutional Critique to productive systems' interfaces. A productive system's interface is the first and last element its facilitator is singularly responsible for.

b. The Relations that occur between participants, viewers and/or administrators of the system should be judged qualitatively.

Nicolas Bourriaud's theory of Relational Aesthetics – the idea that intersubjective encounters are a source of aesthetic worth – automatically comes to mind with this proclamation. However, these relations should be tethered to Claire Bishop's criticism that when approaching Relational Aesthetics, viewers should consider the quality of the relations participants have formed in response to the conditions set forth by the facilitating artist [3]. This requires an analysis of the degree to which participants are able to interact with one another as well as the types of interactions they choose to engage in light of those opportunities. On the internet, it may also be helpful to consider the quantity of participants utilizing a system to understand how relations are effected by digital group dynamics. A critical understanding of Relational Aesthetics in these productive systems should not be based purely on economic or moral standards, which is to say, a system that is well trafficked and features polite banter between participants is not, in itself, necessarily an intriguing work of art. Instead, forms of interaction and participation must be contrasted with the system's interface, raising the possibility that a productive system totally abandoned may provide as much Relational value through its lack of users as a system buzzing with use offers through its masses. The disuse of a productive system may point to an incongruity between the ideology the interface proposes and that of its viewing audience or target demographic of users. Through their absence, a rough sketch of what an audience *does* value may be formed in opposition to a given system.

Following the common belief that the value of art is located in its ability to make visible the previously unseen conditions of existence, what is of Relational value in productive systems may depend upon their users' ability to tactically make use of a structure they did not create – to reveal a responsive model of social operation and regained agency in the production and dispersion of art. Conversely, the embattled relations a productive system fosters may expose what is repressed through the incessant public congeniality of the professionalized art world or other everyday encounters.

c. The artworks produced by participants in a productive system are intrinsically collaborative and aspire towards becoming a common for universal use.

What complicates the 1990's-born theory of Relational Aesthetics when applied to contemporary projects is that the Relations between today's participants are not created by attending events hosted in a museum, but through the communal production of visual works with fellow (internationally-based) artists online in real time, many of whom are producing art in response to one another and/or directives set forth by the system itself. If Conceptual Art provided a framework for viewers to psychically complete a work in any location however they chose based on a set of visual or textual cues left to interpretation, productive systems invite participants to create their own work so others may continuously re-purpose it within the same site of interaction. These visual-conceptual contributions to systems (images, text, html objects, videos, etc.) are collaborative both before and after their initial display. A participant's submitted content is made with the limitations and freedoms of an interface in mind, linking the intentions of the system's facilitator and an artist using that system prior to the submitted work's existence.

After a participant has inserted her visual art in a productive system, it immediately becomes a source material for the use of others through their ability to download the file. The productive systems this essay pertains to also allow participants to variously comment, vote, delete, or reroute whatever has been included by others, making the perception and existence of a work one mutually determined by its community of participatory peers. Such art recalls the notion of a *common*, a term defined by Michael Hardt and Antonio Negri as being a mutually produced resource available to all [4]. A common is not valued according to its profitability in trade, but by its functionality in use. For example, communicative language is a common only as valuable as its ability to be used expressively. When a common is economically or governmentally regulated, it loses the ability to be mutually produced and the incentive to participate with equal agency in its state of becoming is lost. Of course a common must exist within some boundary of formalized recognition, or its purpose would go unnoticed (i.e. a dictionary alerts us to the existence and intended meaning of words so we may use them and knowingly participate in their repurposing).

In the context of art history, the definition of the word 'medium' shares a functional ambivalence with Hardt and Negri's 'common'; each is a placeholder for the relatively open determination of its use by external actors. One may view high modernist art critics' categorical distinctions between mediums as an attempt to establish a set of commons for material production and critical validation. As such, no single person would own 'painting,' but by instituting a universal conception of aesthetic purity and beauty for specific types of making, each artist would have a common basis to challenge or confirm those given principals. After the theoretical collapse of medium specificity, mediums did not disappear but took on an intellectual instead of material form. Rather than establishing their interests within a set of codified physical parameters, such as those of painting or drawing, many post World War II artists chose a subject matter or theory to be versioned and repeated across all different materials and modes of production. As a result, things like pop celebrity or post-structuralism became the 'mediums' in which artists worked and the objects or devices used to visualize those 'mediums' were often a means to a conceptually focused end.

In the absence of standardized modes of material production and the corresponding loss of definitive artistic movements, the desire to produce one's very own 'medium' has been a recurring ambition of artists to differentiate themselves for a variety of reasons. In the case of much art made prior to the 1990's, establishing a medium resulted from repeating one's self. For instance, Ed Ruscha's medium of humorous irreverence was verified through his continued focus on the drawl of roadside Americana. By comparing the unifying dead pan of his many billboard-inspired text paintings or his out-of-the-window photographs of the Hollywood strip, a viewer could eventually identify a set of conceptual interests specific to Ed Ruscha, valuing both his intellectual medium and the artist himself based on their definitive uniqueness. The paradox of this situation is that by repetitively establishing a medium or common conceptual subject for consideration under the guise of a single identity, an artist limits the number of creators for whom it is applicable to one person: herself.

Nicolas Bourriaud describes a turn in the formation of artistic commons towards a tendency he calls Postproduction, whereby the value of an artwork is not located in its ability to be repeated and identified with an individual, but found in its subject matter's capacity to be diversely re-imagined among a network of other artists [5]. To this effect, in their 1999 project, *No Ghost Just A Shell*, Pierre Huyghe and Philippe Parreno invited a number of artists to make use of a manga character named AnnLee whose copyrights they had previously purchased. Also around this time, an internet-specific type of common entered the public lexicon: the meme. Just as today's pop cultural memes are understood based on an alchemy of page views and remixed versions, viewers of contemporary internet art value the repetition of projects through the effort of their peers' reblogs and reproductions. The easiest way to expedite this process of peer awareness and potential recirculation is for an artist to join a pre-existing productive system. Because peers in a productive system recognize the inherently collaborative nature of art placed in this context, posting 'original content' is not an attempt to assert one's uniqueness but a jest made with hopes for a response. Think of it as the slow dialectic process of art history's participants reacting to one another (typified by Robert Rauschenberg's *Erased De Kooning* of 1953) sped up to real time.

While art history has always privileged works that inspired the response of future generations, this collapse of time on the internet has made peer reaction transparent and automatic. Due to the intention among many internet artists to set off a meme-like chain of reaction, a contribution of visual art within a productive system must be evaluated by its salience among peers and ability to thematically reproduce itself. A successful visual work, in this case, is not only defined by its signifiers relative to its conceptual reasoning, but through the ability of the work to act as a 'medium' or common ground for a digital audience of peers to then make use of. Each work that re-purposes and stems outward from an original visual post fosters a self-validating effect. The original is now valuable because it is applicable to its constituents and the remix is valuable because it (hopefully) complicates the idea previously set forth by the original. With each responsive post stemming outward from their initial starting points, the totality of these interrelated artworks take on a rhizomatic shape, growing to be a dynamic common (or multiple commons) for others' conceptual use. One may think of this type of art as an organism, not a product. An artwork's ability to cultivate attention was once an after-the-fact consideration of its social existence. For art displayed in productive systems, it is now a pre-condition of its content's quality.

2. Administrative Cause

A form of art that initiates the production of art by other artists is an admittedly difficult idea at face value. It is even more difficult to consider why these projects typify our current moment, though both become easier to understand when productive systems' facilitators are contextualized through art history and current technology. One way of rationalizing why these systems are being made at this time would be to project upon them what Jaron Lanier calls "the race to be most meta," a term used to describe the competition between Web 2.0 social communication companies to be the most expansive and useful [6]. The logic is that if website A can produce an interface to aggregate what you would do on websites B and C separately, then you have lost the reason to go to websites B and C in the first place, hence, website A has emerged victorious among users through its efficiency. As such, companies like Google and Facebook want to act as the lens through which everyone views and interacts on the internet at all times. It is ubiquity that provides their value. Some may suggest facilitators of productive systems have followed such companies' suit in understanding value through participatory necessity instead of guarded scarcity. The artist who makes her productive system necessary for other art to function has, in a sense, aggregated all of her participants' work through her own interfacial conditions. However, this rationalization is only as applicable as today's facilitators have motives synonymous with those of social media companies. The history and culture surrounding art is certainly competitive, but not limited to profit or growth alone in its motivations.

A similar "race to be most meta" has been feverishly occurring in art's history for over a century. Movements and individuals have continuously revoked the necessity of their predecessors' interests in production by proposing increasingly ontological concerns to which art may be applied. Marcel Duchamp's readymades were a way of announcing:

Before any formal considerations, you must contextually establish a work of art as being such through its location and author. By placing an autographed shovel in a gallery, the artist is, by way of absurdist reduction, making apparent the necessary conditions for value all art must oblige.

Likewise, feminist art of the 1970's was a way of stating:

Before any authorial considerations, you must recognize the subjugation of women in (art) history and the ensuing biases their historical absence has promoted in you as a viewer. My art makes apparent the misogyny entrenched in art's system of value.

This non-stop peeling back of analytic layers has foolishly led artists like the Stuckists to impossibly claim to work outside of the concerns of recent art history. Others are aware of art's expanding considerations, yet choose to ignore them anyway. This is a method that, oddly enough, can alternately lead artists to be considered 'conservative' or oppositely as 'bad boys/girls' based on their ethical positions for doing so. Today's most successful 'conservative' portrait painter is no doubt aware of Duchamp's readymade, though she likely chooses to engage classical portrait painting because of her affection for its history and formal qualities. She is 'conservative' because her work has not expanded alongside her critical moment due to a sincere passion for past methods. Andy Warhol regressively claimed to make art for the sake of making money, an obvious ethical affront to art's proposed self-expressive purity. His more-than-likely awareness of these ethics and subsequent decision to challenge them through meditated provocation made him a 'bad boy' because he knew better but did it his way instead.

Beyond these personas of art making, Boris Groys offers another, more recent development:

> [...] the artist announces the death of the author, that is, his or her own symbolic death. In this case, the artist does not proclaim himself or herself to be bad, but to be dead. The resulting artwork is then presented as being collaborative, participatory, and democratic. [7]

If we are to believe Groys, here art reaches its greatest point of reductive absurdity yet, as though his hypothetical artist says:

Before all else, you must consider your own intention because I didn't make this art and am already dead.

In this situation, it may appear that the dead author is the most sophisticated because she evades artistic criticism and is able to profit from the labor of her minion-like participants. However, it would be as flawed to assign all artistic 'credit' to productive systems' initial facilitators as it would be to say that a skyscraper is singularly understood according to the vision of its architect, and withstands no perceptual influence from the companies, employees, and products that come to realize the building's preliminary design. Identifying these systems solely by their facilitator overlooks what is most inventive about their existence in the first place: *the mutual production of artistic content and value.* As previously reasoned, there *is* a set of criteria capable of addressing productive systems, and the tendency to associate such projects solely with their facilitator is a perceptual error that will hopefully be reconsidered in favor of their participants' efforts.

There is yet another possible intention that is made evident through productive systems' facilitators' actions: the desire to create utopian institutions for art. Consider this – artists were previously (and continue to be) limited by the physicality of their art objects because they required money to reproduce and to store. Digital artists are now able to endlessly reproduce and store infinite amounts of their work at significantly lower costs. This technological shift poses many questions for the internet artist. For example, what possibilities arise when our limitations take the form of time as opposed to more physical limitations like space and material resources?

The artist-produced systems this essay describes have innovatively utilized digital non-space on their own accord. Each of these productive systems presents a major departure in the way their interfaces propose art should be shown or made compared to the rules embodied by traditional institutions. While museums display art linearly or chronologically, there exists a productive system that chaotically presents viewers with a uniquely ordered series of videos every time they enter the site based on a network of textual tags. If art world professionals tend to believe the best art is rooted in finding one's voice through history and practice, today exists a productive system that proposes artists' begin solving each other's artistic dilemmas through joint internships. While museums' curators and boards decide what art is seen in their space, many productive systems' participants decide for one another what art is seen and when through voting and peer aggregation. In light of opportunities made available on the internet for decentralized and low-cost participation, productive systems may be seen as the embodiments of their facilitators' and participants' hopes for how art would most ideally be dispersed and created. While former Institutional Critics attempted to dismantle the master's house using his own tools, productive systems are now using the master's tools to build their own shed in the backyard – not far from home, but definitely outside.

To the facilitators and participants of productive systems, finding holes in the operating methods of the past through written criticism alone is irrelevant – his is a time to create and participate in institutions of their own making. Productive systems literalize methods of operation for artists beyond the normative art world's standards of participation, visibility, individual agency and property. It's growingly apparent something distinct in art's history is happening here, and it is neither to the credit of people or technology alone, but the product of both working in harmony with one another towards a new, radical potential.

2011. Originally published in *491*.

[1] Langdon Winner, "Do Artifacts Have Politics?", in *Daedalus*, Vol. 109, No. 1, Winter, 1980. P. 121.
[2] Ibid., p. 128.
[3] Claire Bishop, "Antagonism and Relational Aesthetics", in *October*, No. 110, Fall 2004. P. 79.
[4] Michael Hardt, Antonio Negri, *Commonwealth*, Belknap Press of Harvard University Press, 2009.
[5] Nicolas Bourriaud, *Postproduction*, Lukas and Sternberg, New York 2002. p. 6.
[6] Jaron Lanier, *You Are Not a Gadget*, Randomhouse, 2010. p. 22.
[7] Boris Groys, "Self Design and Aesthetic Responsibility", in *e-flux journal*, No. 7, June-August 2009. p. 6.

Screens on Screens (Ben Schumacher)

The story about the liquid added to public pools that turns urine into an obvious blue color (mapping the perpetrator's bodily fluids as far as they drift) is actually an urban myth used to deter people from the thought of peeing in pools. It is, however, a decent way to begin thinking about Ben Schumacher's art. The drift of images and objects through the internet is a process silently contested, and many of Schumacher's projects aim to destabilize or re-identify the seemingly normalized flow of digital information as it takes place in social networks. Schumacher has likened his efforts to re-acquaint the online audience with their viewing context in a way parallel to Brancusi's interest in bringing attention to the pedestals on which his sculptures sat. For an artist whose practice tends toward the disclosure of unforeseen linkages, this historical referent is definitely fitting.

Embracing the altered nature of installation images when placed on his blog, Schumacher [1] often overlays Photoshopped brushstrokes and signatures on his imagery; a gesture at once recognizing the object-turned-image's new status as a flattened visual artifact while also self-effacingly acknowledging the transience of authorship in the images' new digital environment. The sentiment forms that there are a number of people being attributed authorship to his work, an act that is perhaps pre-empting the many contexts a single image may be viewed through once part of the labyrinth of Tumblrs and image aggregates that exist. In a related project [2], Schumacher tracks the way people disperse his imagery through their own blogs, but here too the context Schumacher is interested in is multiple as well. In these screen grabbed images of his work being posted on other blogs, the artist includes a full view of his own desktop, revealing a new cast of browser tabs, installed software icons and floating files each time. This twice-removed view of Schumacher coming to terms with his own work is offered up for further transcription and re-blogging on Tumblr, again revealing a willingness to absolve himself as the known creator and an interest in re-couping what happens when he does so. To this point, it should make sense that the artist has no collection of work online that is not a Blogspot or Tumblr archive, using only active platforms with built-in features for appropriation. Schumacher has even dabbled in posting his work on little known image hosting websites, noting the results as each of the image repositories slowly go bankrupt or are swallowed by larger companies.

They say if you love something you should set it free, and if it loves you back it will return: enter Schumacher's work with the trading sites eBay and Craigslist. For his 2010 JstChillin project the artist openly propositioned 3D modelers on Craigslist to digitally replicate installation images of his sculptures. To his surprise, a number of modelers returned his query with modeled designs for free. Some responses were stamped with watermarks and messages from their creators urging Schumacher to pay them to receive the watermark-free version of their 3D modeled image. Schumacher obliged, maintaining an archive of his own installation images, the free versions offered by Craigslist modelers, the watermarked versions and the un-watermarked versions given after payment. The result is a body of images that both seamlessly blend and bluntly differ in appearance, highlighting (in some instances) the possibility for flawless digital simulation and in others the unsettled artifacts of labor negotiations. As Schumacher has said about textual scholars:

What becomes apparent through the reading of printed variants of the original file is not only differences in the modes of production but the subjective behavior of the authors of the variants who will the original file into existence.

Names like Luna, Christopher Perez, and Belartist appear prominently as fingerprints left by red-blooded creators at the helm of technology indifferently geared towards leveling all difference in digital versus real comparisons. It is a quiet, though conceptually effective gesture that Schumacher always returns his compensated 3D models to Google Warehouse, an offering made as repayment at the altar of digital collaboration.

For his work on eBay, Schumacher has taken to sending car door windows at random, straight from the online marketplace, to unsuspecting individuals who have done studio visits with him. Without mention of whom the object is from or why they have received it, recipients often take a cell phone image of the object and message it to Schumacher and others in their phone book searching for the window's sender. In an eloquent reversal of the aforementioned Craigslist's works' driving force being the negotiation of labor metted through censorial names, here the lack of an authorial signature actually propels the dispersion of images sent through mobile phones. Schumacher collects these cell phone images, along with the installation views offered on eBay and 3-D models he's had his most trusted Craigslist workers create of the car door windows to form a layered viewing of an as-of-yet-virtual object Schumacher himself has never seen in person.

Similarly, the artist credits an interest in the mythical notion of Acheiropoieta – the idea of an icon not made by the human hand, such as the Veil of Veronica or the Shroud of Turin – as being a motivating force behind his use of 3D printing as a sculptural process and material. Schumacher says:

> Scanning software used to map large areas of terrain enters the world simultaneously with the time of their production and denies any notion of subject or subjective gaze. The formerly irreducible time between an event and it's inscription in the world is reduced to 0 and the subject (of enunciation and operation) has disappeared... Like Acheiropoieta, there now exists representation that functions autonomously, independent of human intervention and inscription.

Ironically the 3D printing technology Schumacher employs cannot help but manifest its own 'fingerprint' on its products. The green to purple tie-dyed color apparent on these Google 3D Warehouse-sourced objects is not the result of a gothic-hippie taste of Schumacher's own, but of a breakdown in communication between the printers' input and output. Due to the additive coloring process currently used by 3D printers (layering levels of cyan, magenta and yellow atop one another) black is a color unable to be printed by the machines, despite the information Schumacher includes in his files commanding the objects to be colored so. The resulting green to purple mist on the objects' surface is, by design standards, a failure, though by artistic standards reveals a compelling glance at the medium's inability to not interfere with the message. Or, as Schumacher says:

> a digital model produced and printed in 2009 can have the exact same form as the same file printed in 2050; however, the physical objects themselves may differ in their material qualities and precision due to constantly updated printing technologies.

The notion of signatures (consciously made or otherwise) is never far off in Schumacher's work.

Just as 3D prints are essentially objects representing virtual images (a reversal of our traditional understandings of representation relative to materiality), so too do Schumacher's paintings strive to switch our perceptions of viewing order. A close look at his canvases shows a rugged cement base with enamel drizzled over at an extreme angle, as though dust had accumulated on them for centuries in a world of oblique gravity. From a distance this aging process reverses and the canvases' abstract subject matter appears in hyper-contemporary style, identical to any number of the Photoshop-produced and Chinese-printed digital paintings that have become so popular recently. Like the simultaneously failed and generative surface of his 3D prints, Schumacher's paintings use materiality to gesture towards an idealized future of representation. The ancient grit of cement appears to be a suitable form for seemingly 'digital' graphics, until the viewer steps too far to the right, left or approaches it too closely – then the facade crumbles under material limitation.

Perhaps in Schumacher we have found a truly Post-Internet artist, actively blending virtual and material information through transfer and documentation. Leaping from physical appearance to digital representation, known authorship to anonymity, or technological objectivity to the human hand, Schumacher's art achieves interconnectivity in a way that transcends the rhetoric of a word used all too often.

2011. Originally published in *Dis Magazine*.

[1] Cf. http://worse.tumblr.com.
[2] Cf. http://schumachercollage.tumblr.com.

Why You Should Make Yourself Someone Else Online

Among the many things you will learn by watching the Ondi Timoner-directed documentary film *WE LIVE IN PUBLIC*, you will discover that Josh Harris became a millionaire in the early 1990's by selling a beta version of chat room software to Prodigy. He then took his millions and started the raucous Pseudo.com, a silicon alley social media company that pioneered streaming video and niche-personalized online content creation. Harris's penchant for frequently dressing up as an effeminate clown in corporate settings and general lack of business savvy forced him to move on from Pseudo. Throughout the film Harris' intentions never seemed to align with those of a businessman so much as a provocateur. One of the ways Harris felt he could best provoke the status quo was by eliminating the communicative distance that separated people from one another online. Harris so firmly believed in abolishing the lines between media distribution and media consumption that he predicted (either through an invention of his own or someone else's) we would each become the sites of production for others' media experience, consensually opening our lives to surveillance in exchange for the warmth of attention and communal validation. Not a bad guess.

Harris's belief in peer to peer consensual surveillance was continued through his dystopic technological concentration camp and socially engineered conceptual art project *Quiet: We Live in Public*. In 1999 Harris bought an underground Soho building where he equipped pre-approved residents with the ability to spy on each other at all times while giving them access to food and all other life necessities for free in addition to a fully equipped gun range, drugs and see-through showers. After *Quiet...* was busted by the police on New Years Day 2000 under suspicions of being a heavily armed religious cult, Josh Harris switched projects and chose himself as his next subject. Soon after, Harris moved in to an apartment rigged for 24 hour surveillance broadcast through the internet with his girlfriend Tanya Corrin and for the following several months participated in the now-offline project *weliveinpublic.com*.

As the dot com bubble's burst ruined his finances and his relationship became increasingly isolated and occasionally violent, Harris's life unraveled before the eyes of his live, online audience. Viewers of this spectacle were able to discuss the events they watched through a chatroom placed next to the surveillance video on the weliveinpublic.com website. What most interested me about this process was the way in which both Harris and Corrin ceased to interact directly with each other and came to understand their relationship through the proxy of the duo's online chat room reception. After every fight the couple ran to their respective computers to monitor how their online audience interpreted who won the fight or who was in the wrong. Even in the beginning of the project when the couple wasn't fighting many of their actions were rewarded or occasionally instigated by their online audience. As the audience came to fall out of favor with Harris and increasingly went on to back Corrin's thoughts about leaving him, so too dissolved their relationship.

While peer-mediated digital communication does allow access to multiple viewpoints and the possibility to gain greater wisdom from a diversity of interpretations, there are some serious downsides to this way of understanding reality. A subject who is being 'purely' surveilled is not aware of those watching her and proceeds to act in a natural way. Pure surveillance is a one-way glass that allows many to be aware of the actions of one with no possibility for reciprocation. Once this pact has been broken, and the subject is made aware of her own status as a recorded image being watched by an other, she becomes a performer intrinsically linked to the will of her audience. For someone aware of the fact they are being watched but are without the ability to directly communicate with those watching them, the typical response is to abide by whatever the performer believes to be the most widely agreed upon conception of morality or good behavior. Don't steal on camera, don't pick your nose, don't pull out your wedgie –

they're watching. This performance is what Michael Foucault describes as the internalization of discipline. When someone is being surveilled and *does* have the ability to directly communicate with the people surveilling her (as was the case in *weliveinpublic.com*'s live-streaming chat room), the mode of performance such a person enters becomes more fluid – morality is determined by the Pavlovian reward and punishment system of her audience. Assuming the number of people in direct communication with the surveilled subject are real (that the accounts in the chat room aren't all the same person pretending to be different people), there is an inherent asymmetry in the way this dialogue works.

By seeking the approval of the online audience surveilling them, Harris and Corrin lost a bit of their humanity by externalizing their decision making process to a largely anonymized digital mass of people. In return, they gained peer validated understandings of reality, lessening the discomfort of acting according to their own subjectivity. There is a mutual exchange of power in this process between Harris and his audience, but it is a lopsided one. Not only is the crowd in an unequal position of leverage (one versus hundreds), but within that crowd exists certain social dynamics able to easily tip which way the majority's opinion will fall. When communicating online, people have a tendency of projecting their previous notions of conversational structure into a new environment that doesn't match it. This rear view understanding of the future is present all over our computers' interfacial language, where we place imaginary 'files' into imaginary 'folders' and use cursors that look like imaginary 'hands' to visit imaginary 'pages' – all office terms of the past used to explain the work environment of the present and future. The same goes for how we communicate with each other, expecting the way we chat online to match up with the way we previously did in person. Some differences in communication have made themselves readily apparent; we didn't previously speak to one another based on 140 character limits. Other differences are less obvious, and can be explained by the way anonymity effects our proclivity for dissent.

Anonymity has long provided a safe harbor for dissent, from the trope of the nameless whistleblower to the witness protection plan. Institutions formed to protect the anonymity of those with contrarian information were used to shield the dissenter from retaliation at the hands of whomever the dissenter was threatening to reveal. In these courtroom instances anonymity was a necessary measure of protection because the dissenter was in a weakened position to confront a jury. In general, we grant these witnesses a certain amount of credibility because they are willing to sacrifice their own safety and potentially the future of their identity to release information they believe to be crucial for the sake of justice. Another place where institutions are formed to create anonymous dialogue is on the internet – though this kind of digital anonymity works opposite of how it does in a courtroom. On the internet, the tables have turned, and in a chatroom like *weliveinpublic.com*'s, the anonymous mass is the majority and the named individual is the minority. If the idealized form of what the witness protection plan allows for is the whistle blowing employee, the normalized form of what the internet's anonymity allows for is the comment thread troll.

The troll is a kamikaze-esque figure; often sacrificing her own image's good standing within a community and/or the civility of discourse to achieve her desired effect of perceptual disruption. The troll does not wish to join the conversation so much as she wishes to take those with the false pretension or actual possession of power in a discourse down a peg. When trolling takes the form of written text, this kind of disruption is accomplished by inserting the most dimly divisive material into a conversation possible or resorting to personal attacks. For this reason, trolls have a tendency of nit-picking minor details, using 'snark' in place of research, and conflating the content of a speaker's ideas with what they perceive to be the content of that speaker's character. Trolls can be demonstrably incorrect in what they pass off as facts because conversational truth or consensus is not what they intend on achieving. As Momus said, "Every lie creates a parallel world, the world in which it's true." [1] In a populist digital environment, lies and disinformation are able to travel at light speeds, giving a new dimension to the old idea of "if its printed, it's true". The troll is aware of this fact, and often produces disinformation that hovers just at the cusp of believability.

And Like a kamikaze fighter the troll is also a rational actor, believing her actions – no matter how self-destructive or slanderous they are at the moment – justify her ends and ultimately reward her afterwards. This reward has often been summed up as "doing it for the lulz" – which is true in some online environments – but is not the only intended result for other forms of trolling. In fact, *any* zealotry can be expressed through trolling, be it political, personal or even artistic difference.

Trolls do not have to be anonymous, though it helps in their tactical process. Many trolls actually work with their real names, taking advantage of a paradox of (dis)embodiment many users perceive in their internet use. To explain this paradox simply, internet users often believe the form their communication takes place through (a chatroom, for instance) is not a 'real' version of communication, while simultaneously believing the content they acquire in those 'unreal' digital environments is or can be true. It is this cognitive disconnect that allows sarcastic sayings like "Where'd you learn that? *Wikipedia*?" to be popular alongside the religious devotion people have to celebrity gossip blogs. We forget the named messenger, but keep the troll's message anyway.

Considering it's inequalities and the potential for trolls to wreak havok, online surveillance has been given a bad name – and rightfully so. The most common associations we have with surveillance are with projects designed to regulate the behavior of a group of people (prisons, road traffic cameras, church confessionals) or to spy on their private actions so to become more familiar with their desires for the purchase of selling those desires back to them profitably (Google AdSense, Facebook, market demographic research). In both cases, the reason for our unease toward surveillance results from the uneven power dynamic created when one party is able to opaquely determine or monitor the actions of another party without their consent. One of the most publicized stories in recent history has dealt very specifically with surveillance, but not in the top-down sense we have come to associate it with. Wikileaks is a surveillance program with intentions to monitor the secretive dealings of the world's political and financial elites. It's an epic irony that the same governing and military bodies who have relentlessly pursued an agenda of increased human surveillance domestically and abroad now find the surveillance of their own actions a terrorizing threat. Wikileaks provides a counter-example to prevailing norms, showing that surveillance can be positive practice when it seeks to level the inequalities of political power by increasing the transparency of private debates that have extremely public consequences. Think of it as a surveillance for the people instead of a surveillance of the people.

In his essay *Why Things Matter*, Julian Bleecker describes a blogosphere growingly in dialogue with inanimate or non-human things producing loads of informative content. Bleecker offers the example of a project called *The Pigeon that Blogs* by Beatriz da Costa where a flock of pigeons, equipped with GPS devices and chemical monitoring sensors designed to record the levels of toxins and pollutants in the air, are released to fly all over and report back the "current toxic state of the local atmosphere" in real time online. Once again, here a largely invisible process – pollution – is given a real face and the documentation to prove it. Bleecker goes on to describe other potentially liberating models of surveillance that could aid the public, saying:

> **What if our RSS aggregators could tune into feeds from Amazonian forest and the daily clear-cut blog? Or critter cam video blogs that show us how really nasty seal bulls can be to**

their pups when they're not playing their circus act at Sea World. And video blogs from schools of dolphins and whales that will make it increasingly difficult to ignore the plumes of toxins in the oceans and the slaughter of their kin by whalers and felonious fishing fleets. [2]

To apply these environmental ideas of surveillance to the context of art, the only thing more cynical and perverse than the web of dealers, institutional officials and artists implicated in the 2010 New Museum insider trading fiasco revolving around Jeff Koons and his collector Dakis Joannou (as heavily publicized and revealed through the blogosphere) was the all too common response of jaded commentators who claimed that the subject was unworthy of attention because of how rampant this kind of inside trading is in the art world. It was as though Tyler Green was telling a group of WWE fanatics professional wrestling wasn't real, despite everyone's awareness that it's not. Artists with ambitions of operating in the market – much like WWE fans – must proceed with some level of suspension of disbelief that art's bureaucracy of institutional validation functions as a meritocracy and not a profit-driven cesspool of aristocratic reach arounds cleverly disguised as high culture. To think otherwise would be a denigration of one's *own* work if it were to ever become market successful.

When information obtained through surveillance is distributed in an egalitarian fashion it forces us to confront facts about our lives and the people we know – facts that are often buried by others to hide their wrongdoing or buried by ourselves to make life more convenient at the cost of our own integrity. As mentioned, surveillance can do good if it's not just used to re-enforce existing societal dynamics, but instead used to shake up and expose the inequities of those relations. One thing for certain is that surveillance – both the good and bad kinds – will continue to grow to be an ever-present force in our public and private lives. Like the rapid spread of computers and mobile devices to the developing world, ideas and products that are advantageous to the health of global capitalism will continue to reproduce themselves. Additionally, so long as there remains a will for openness in our political processes there will remain a desire for the surveillance of politicians in a way more meaningful than the endless number of C-Spans available. Both the profit-hungry corporation and the accountability-demanding citizen want greater transparency, and the internet is a place they both can agree they will find the hidden information they are looking for about one another.

In the social world of the internet this means we must cherish and protect our ability to consensually choose what information we are associated with in the eyes of others. Online brand making is the new art of the masses – it is the only process of aesthetic construction America's population almost universally shares. The capacity to manipulate and construct an identity online separate from our everyday existence is an expression of freedom from totalizing surveillance that would automatically provide information on our behalf. It is a slippage in the prevailing ideology of Facebook that users are still able to post their own pictures – or rather, to use images that have nothing to do with themselves as their profile pictures. If the same ideas of textual, written objectivity inherent in the necessity to use your real name were applied visually, Facebook would have long ago instituted valid photo IDs in the same way they are necessitated by national passports. A true conception of freedom of expression must include the possibility of lying or abstaining from expression altogether. The process of image management on Facebook is already less an outpouring of expression than it is an exercise in *omission* of information about one's self. Which picture will I untag myself from today? I encourage everyone to be more erraticly dishonest – or better, willfully *creative* – when going about constructing a representation of themselves on Facebook. The further you have digitally deviated from your every day existence the better. Your continued honesty in behaving as you truly would without anyone watching is the only way AdSense works. If the parties exposed by Wikileaks are hard at work making sure they become even more opaque in their communication, we too must become equally misleading if we want to keep pace. Chat rooms aren't real places anyway, right?

Written in 2011.

[1] Momus, *The Book of Scotlands*, Sternberg Press, New York 2009.
[2] Julian Bleecker, "A Manifesto for Networked Objects: Cohabiting with Pigeons, Arphids and Aibos in the Internet of Things (Why Things Matter)", self published pdf, undated. P. 16. Online at www.nearfuturelaboratory.com/2006/02/26/a-manifesto-for-networked-objects/.

Tsimulacrum

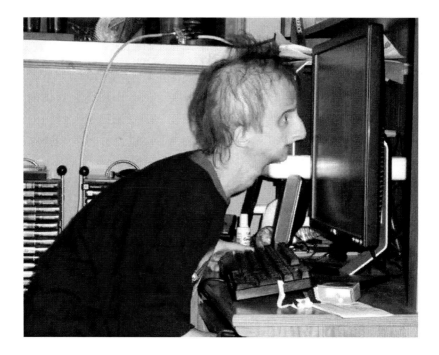

Everyone has seen a Tsimfuckis video. When conversation dulled at a friend's house one night, someone next to you picked up the laptop, paused iTunes and showed you one of his videos. As anticipated, lulz ensued. Or possibly horror. Or sympathy. Probably not empathy. Something happened, though. Waking the next morning alone in a Pabst-smeared haze, unsure of whether what you viewed the night before was what it had played itself out to be, you reached for your Macbook and Googled your best to recreate the magic. Maybe you texted the person who was next to you for searchable clues, but eventually you found him again. Then you saw the numbers below – the millions upon millions of views and comments. What were we all looking for in Tsimfuckis anyway?

Probably the same thing he was looking for. Like us, Justin Tsimbidis, aka Tsimfuckis, aka Tsimbigis, aka Chickenlittl3, of Corona, New York, has watched a lot of MTV and YouTube videos. The most surreptitious aspect of popular media is that it rarely gives us answers to our lives' conundrums, though it often structures our expectations for how things should be. Having been trapped in a feedback loop since 1992, the Real World my generation lives in is one sleekly portrayed as more honest than the generation before it. This time, the party's invite CC'ed every minority identity under the sun – and despite being snubbed for the past century of mass media, they all showed up in person! It was definitely good fun, everyone there was amplified on Red Bull, clarified on Proactiv and terrified when hang gliding in Tijuana. We all hung out for days on end, high on the thrill of just seeing one another for the first time. Eventually Pedro and Coral and Ruthie became our new gay, black, and drug-addicted friends, respectively. But something was missing.

The Real became an itch we just couldn't scratch, so we dug even deeper. A cottage industry was dedicated to the pursuit of finding it. Every night we became friends with even more locked up prisoners, hoarders, and canned air huffers. We stopped being polite, but somehow things felt even less satisfying. For each new friend we made a void was created. The edited display of popular media defined our anticipations for how to treat its subjects. Watching good Southern guys and bad girls clubs weren't subterranean explorations so much as they were polished presentations. With every quick cut and planned musical accompaniment we were given a cheat sheet for how to feel and afterwards we felt bad for getting an A.

The larger (though related) problem was that we knew all along it wasn't Real – no surprise there, we've been suspending our disbelief for decades now. Not because our new best friends were too talented or pretty, but simply because they were too interesting. Reality is really, really boring. You, reading this in your surplus of time, are or were likely bored. I too am boring, though have the advantage of editing what I say to you in a punchy, direct manner. What is Real about Youtube is that – for the grand majority – it sucks. We have become so fickle in our understanding of reality relative to entertainment that anything too watchable mustn't be true. This pairing of viewed enjoyment conflated with falseness makes us loathe ourselves for indulging our own attention spans. Irony is helpful in that it bridges the gap between what we hate and what we enjoy, allowing its practitioners brief immunity from a pursuit of what is Real, but it doesn't resolve the question altogether so much as it puts the question off to be answered another day, or by another person.

Tsimfuckis' videos hit a sweet spot in our understanding of Real entertainment because he was able to introduce us to a new type of tweenage friend (the kind that has Progeria) and a form of content we know as objective (the boring kind). This second part cemented Tsimfuckis' role as a Real person and meme celebrity – the relentless monotony inherent in his own process of making and any viewer's process of watching his videos. For proof of this claim, I'd recommend readers watch all of Tsimfuckis's video *Fight with a Pillow*, a video of 350,000+ views wherein he performs WWE-style wrestling moves on a New York Yankees pillow on top of his bed in complete silence for a total of two minutes and twenty five seconds before giving the pillow a 3 count and yelling his own name in victory before turning the camera off. One gets the sense that the pillow battle was the final stop in a search for possible video options, an event created for the sake of creation alone. An unintentional masterpiece of our generation, *Fight with a Pillow*'s aimless rivalry (man versus pillow) perfectly mirrors Tsimfuckis's own viewers' circular quarrels with one another regarding the proper moral tone to address a person stricken with Progeria. The comment threads below Tsimfuckis's videos reveal an audience stripped of their reactionary instructions, left to their own devices to sort through how to respond to a young person with a life-threatening disease camwhoring. Once the dichotomy of 'moral fagging' (shaming others on the basis of popular morality) versus hateful trolling (making fun of a kid with Progeria) was established through a load of sympathy videos and prank commentary, clever trolls secretly switched their position to being overzealous moral fags in an attempt to bait the angered response of lesser trolls. Throughout this process of trolls trolling trolls, Tsimfuckis himself faded into the background and his videos became a stadium for the athletic pursuit of communal annoyance. The snake began nibbling on itself, and for a few moments everyone was able to stave off the hunger pangs of boredom.

2011. Originally published in *Dis Magazine*.

In Response to 'Dispersion' by Seth Price

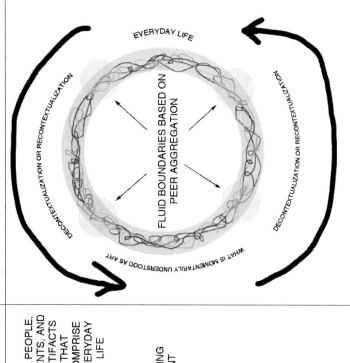

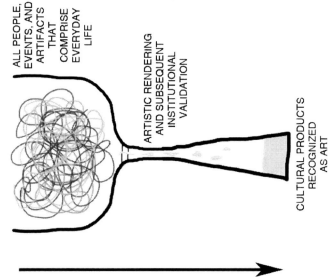

After reading the essay *Dispersion* [1], I'm certain Seth Price knows plenty about the history of conceptual art. In the essay Price mentions the failure of an obscure invention by Marcel Duchamp, quotes the largely forgotten Joseph Kosuth-edited publication *The Fox*, and rarely goes more than 4 pages without a Dan Graham reference of some kind. Images of artworks are tucked away in corners and between paragraphs everywhere you look. Today, my peers tend to view this writing as seminal, making it required reading among their students and partly dedicating museum exhibitions to it. With such community support I thought maybe this time I would finally sort through Price's maze of citations and find a message to band around. I was surprisingly disappointed to find the author's message for the future was essentially a nihilistic one: *Resistance Is Futile*.

The third page of *Dispersion* begins:

> What would it mean to step outside of this carefully structured system? Duchamp's *Rotorelief* experiment stands as a caution, and the futility of more recent attempts to evade the institutional system has been well documented.

In a similar tone, he states in the essay's second-to-last paragraph:

> An art that attempts to tackle the expanded field, encompassing arenas other than the standard gallery and art world-circuit, sounds utopian at best and possibly naive and undeveloped [...]

In some ways, maybe Seth Price is right. Maybe it is impossible to entirely leave the art institutions we have. All of this talk needs some clarification, though. Which point does Price refer to in his description of institutional departure – before a work is made or at the moment it is presented to the public? As artist and theorist Andrea Fraser eloquently states in her essay "Why Does Fred Sandback's Work Make Me Cry?" [2]:

> We are all members of cultural fields. We carry, in each of us, our institutions inside ourselves. There's a museum here, inside of me, with the Corinthian columns, the grand staircase, and the mezzanine. [...] Just as art cannot exist outside the field of art, I cannot exist outside the field of art, at least not as what I am, which is an artist.

To this effect, I agree that the canonized history of art is ingrained in my genetic code of creative production. I cannot escape awareness of an inherited understanding of who Marcel Duchamp was any easier than I could forget my own middle name. As an essential component of art's being, the direction and quality of this contextual basis makes the fields of art education and written discourse all the more important, raising crucial questions about how art is taught and to whom.

However, at the moment of presentation, the idea that art can be validated, discussed and displayed through alternate systems than the normative institutions in place is by no means naïve, and already exists in different forms. Price himself conflictingly testifies to this fact, saying:

> [t]he film avant-garde, for instance, has always run on a separate track from the art world, even as its practitioners may have been pursuing analogous concerns.

The reasons why Price, in his own words, believes it is "demonstrably impossible to destroy or dematerialize Art" are twofold. First, he cites the necessity of documentation and its ability to fix meaning, saying:

> [biopolitical art] must depend on a record of its intervention into the world, and this documentation is what is recouped as art, short-circuiting the original intent [of blurring art and life].

This idea – that all art must assume a recorded form of some kind to exist in history is true, but the permanence of any recorded form is not as stable as Price would have readers believe. Words and images (the mediums Price describes as the binding translations of life into art) are only as fixed as the context of those documents remains strictly controlled in time and space. Separate from the architecturally and culturally determined atmosphere of traditional artistic display, documentation of any action or artifact dispersed on the internet – be it artistic or not – is subject to a wide array of distortion, reproduction and reinvention. What is fluid about the contextual environment of the internet translates to the fluidity of meaning for its contents.

Price describes the inevitable home of said documentation to be the *archive*. He mentions the archive with a post-modern flavor of skepticism due to its reliance on "cataloguing, provenance, and authenticity."

Providing an alternative to the archive, Price comes just shy of saying the word 'internet', instead describing a hypothetical "popular archive" that "does not share an administrative tendency". The author continues:

> Suppose an artist were to release the work directly into a system that depends on reproduction and distribution for sustenance, a model that encourages contamination, borrowing, stealing and horizontal blur. The art system usually corrals errant works, but how could it recoup thousands of freely circulating paperbacks?

This question remains unanswered in Price's essay, functioning as a rhetorical device to affirm the futility of a distributional system without administrative moderators. In his book *The Wealth of Networks*, theorist Yochai Benkler describes a similar problem:

> The rst-generation critique of the democratizing effect of the Internet was based on various implications of the problem of information overload, or the Babel objection. According to the Babel objection, when everyone can speak, no one can be heard, and we devolve either to a cacophony or to the reemergence of money as the distinguishing factor between statements that are heard and those that wallow in obscurity. [3]

For Benkler, though, the Babel objection is a conundrum of the past, explaining its resolution as such:

> Users tend to treat other people's choices about what to link to and to read as good indicators of what is worthwhile for them. They are not slavish in this, though; they apply some judgment of their own as to whether certain types of users – say, political junkies of a particular stripe, or fans of a speci c television program – are the best predictors of what will be interesting for them. The result is that attention in the networked environment is more dependent on being interesting to an engaged group of people than it is in the mass-media environment, where moderate interest to large numbers of weakly engaged viewers is preferable. Because of the redundancy of clusters and links, and because many clusters are based on mutual interest, not on capital

> investment, it is more dif cult to buy attention on the Internet than it is in mass media outlets, and harder still to use money to squelch an opposing view. These characteristics save the networked environment from the Babel objection without reintroducing excessive power in any single party or small cluster of them, and without causing a resurgence in the role of money as a precondition to the ability to speak publicly. [4]

In other words, despite the plethora of material online, when a person logs on to the internet, she is not confronted with millions of random posts, comments, and videos all at once. Instead, she most likely checks some source of trusted aggregation first – whether that is her e-mail inbox, an RSS feed reader or other platforms for peer communication. The internet is no more random and structured than a walk down a busy street full of window shops with open doors – the attractions are plentiful, but the path to viewing them requires an intentional engagement. The lack of "corralling" Price laments is simply not a reality with art or any other content online; each internet user is her own organizational strategist. For art on the internet, this has manifested itself in the seemingly endless number of blogs dedicated to collecting and promoting art focused on a variety of subject matters.

The second obstacle in *Dispersion* that Price finds "impossible" for art's foray into everyday life is the insularity of conceptually difficult artworks.

He says:

> Kosuth's quotation from Roget's Thesaurus placed in an *Artforum* ad, or Dan Graham's list of numbers laid out in an issue of *Harper's Bazaar* were uses of mass media to deliver coded propositions to a specialist audience, and the impact of these works, signficant and lasting as they were, reverted directly to the relatively arcane realm of the art system, which noted these efforts and inscribed them in its histories.

Without an embedded awareness of art's history and methods, it is unlikely that all viewers will be able to understand the entirety of a given work of art's potential meanings. If the institution is not "inside of you" there is no way of projecting it outwards or using it as a lens of viewing. However, this does not mean all potential behind a work of art is lost in a public setting. People have an uncanny ability to grasp not just the surface, but also the inner workings of a variety of conceptual Trojan horses. The human capacity to discover, adapt, and repurpose a given environment or artifact to best suit their own goals is the cornerstone of our existence as a species. The art that is most germane to being released in everyday life is that which is able to converse with others on a level that transcends a mere reliance on the codified norms of art history. The internet is rife with art projects that have achieved popularity well exceeding the limits of art audiences alone, from Rafael Rozendaal's interactive sites, to Ann Hisch's *Scandalishious* project, to Chris Collins' *Bad Paintings of Barack Obama*, to Jon Rafman's *Koolaid Man* and *9 Eyes of Google Street View* projects, to David Horvitz's *Head in the Refrigerator* meme, to Miranda July and Harrell Fletcher's *Learning to Love You More* website and on and on.

In Price's defense, there *is* a great amount of insularity in art, stemming from the moments before production to the time of its presentation and beyond. The culture of art is steeped in a tradition of privacy in almost every way imaginable: the studio as an enclosed private space, the privacy of individualized production of art, the art object as a privately owned good, the intellectual privacy granted to those who are making 'art for art's sake', the privacy of artists' research processes in coming to create a work of art, the privacy of art's preparation, the privacy of disclosing large chunks of information about the way art's institutions operate in capitalist markets. On the other hand, if you notice, throughout that (abbreviated) list of private aspects of art, each point mentioned pertained to the creation, contextualization and dispersion of art – not the art itself! This is because art is ideally a communicative medium that strives for the impossible realization of providing its viewers and makers with greater perceptual clarity in the world they inhabit. Art wants to speak to everyone, but it primarily exists in a culture of closed-off scarcity.

In science, evolution only occurs when there is variation in the inherited traits of a population. Disparate gene pools compete to provide genetically coded organisms best suited for the difficulties of their environment. The privacy of art is a regressive example of cultural inbreeding; it is a process that creates weak inventions only suitable for and responsible to rarified historical interests. In nature, inbred organisms are typically killed off by those who have diversely adapted to the world they live in, though in the case of art, this introduction of outside influence has been curtailed by its existence within a bubble of institutional insularity.

The process of introducing art into everyday life (and equally importantly, everyday life into art) is as much about displaying various artifacts to people in different fields of knowledge as it is a pedagogical project of finding and articulating semblance between those divides. I am in total agreement with Price when he says "Some of the most interesting recent artistic activity has taken place outside the art market and its forums," both in terms of the content of non-art-accredited cultural products as well as the innovative structures for dispersion other fields have fostered. And though artists have proven capable of appropriating a wide range of subject matters into their work, what remains unchallenged are the *structural* components of artistic production – the various ongoing privacies mentioned above. These structural traits will also need to be subject to the same processes of translation and adoption of outside methods in a manner as readily as artists appropriate content outside their own history. A digital resistance to institutional norms is not futile – it is absolutely necessary. Extinction, after all, is the reward for those incapable of change.

Written in 2011.

[1] Seth Price, "Dispersion", 2002 – ongoing. Online at www.distributedhistory.com/Dispersion08.pdf.
[2] Andrea Fraser, "Why Does Fred Sandback's Work Make Me Cry?", in *Grey Room*, Winter 2006, No. 22, pp. 30 - 47.
[3] Yochai Benkler, *The Wealth of Networks. How Social Production Transforms Markets and Freedom*, Yale University Press, New Haven and London, p. 10.
[4] Ibid., p. 13.

The Minor League

IMAGE FOR A PROPOSED CHILDREN'S TELEVISION SHOW ABOUT ARTIST PARKER ITO CREATED BY AND POSTED ON ARTIST CHRIS COY'S TUMBLR, 2010

Reflecting on Dutch artist Rafael Rozendaal's chaotically orchestrated Bring Your Own Beamer exhibit at Spencer Brownstone this past weekend, several questions concerning contemporary internet artists have since come to mind. Who are all of these artists, how are they linked and what is their relation to a for-profit venture such as Spencer Brownstone? All readily apparent answers feature a similar conclusion: the internet and market-dominated art worlds are *not* separate entities and will continue to wrap their tentacles around each other as time progresses. Currently, many Web 2.0 artists utilize the internet as a publicity and networking machine with the latent hope of using their social capital accumulated online as an opportunity for commercial exhibition later (or sooner) in life. The distributional efficiency of artists publishing content online can very easily serve as an appendage of the art market. There is already a "minor league" feeder program in the making, where galleries and other institutions discover artists who are digitally popularized. Using a combination of websites including but not limited to Tumblr, Youtube, Delicious and Facebook, these artists are able to produce intricate webs of cross promotion and widespread recognition. The minor league is created by internet-based art communities and market-influenced institutions performing a feedback loop with one another through an intimate understanding of the other's social and economic value.

As a minor league, internet art communities aid commercial galleries by calling attention to artists whose work has garnered an audience people are already interested in, ending the guessing game of whether or not an artist's projects will be palpable to a wider viewership. By increasing her visibility, an artist's digital peers practically elect her to a position in luxury capitalism. In return, all of those peers who previously supported her are bestowed with the social capital of the art gallery's decision making because they had the good sense to help validate someone who was *going places* (though it is unclear how this value can or will ever be translated offline). This is not to mention the likely increased amount of respect an artist's peers will have for her as a result of her gallery approval.

Gallery directors basing their representational decisions on the amount of attention an artist cultivates online is a much less despotic version of capitalism than the case in which directors strictly choose to represent artists based on their perceived profitability among collectors' previously demonstrated tastes. The former takes into account art that is relevant to many people and the latter anticipates the interests of few. This influence from the internet does not equalize the disproportionate amount of power the individual gallery director has in determining the offline public's perception of what art is of merit or solve the gallery's locationally-exclusive problems of viewer access – but it's an improvement on the status quo in at least one regard.

The minor league is not an example of an alternative structure to the art market, but a newly available path to succeeding within it. In the minor league we see the internet's participants and profit-based institutions thriving from one another, exchanging power to embolden themselves through the other's promotional exclusivity. What separates the minor league and its contemporary offline peers is not the ambition to be recognized or to have a career – it's the fact that the former has more successfully engaged a national audience at a younger age than ever before. Several years ago, there was much talk at the peak of the market bubble about whether or not giving barely-graduated artists so much money so early in their careers would be healthy for their state of mind in the long run. While the money may now be absent for most, money's counterpart – attention – has become a permanent staple for internet artists who are even as young as teenagers. To the artists of the Web 2.0 generation, it is accepted that there is never a moment outside the view of one's peers when online. Privacy simply does not exist. It's increasingly difficult to separate the professional and social ties of the minor league, as even personal Facebook accounts are integral to these artists' brands. Once upon a time people rubbed shoulders, now the minor league displays their alliances through public displays of affection on each others' walls and tagged photos. This is not to say they've never met in person – the minor league has traveled across America and beyond, slept on each other's couches and shown their work in each other's apartment galleries. For a group of strangers, the minor league is a surprisingly intimate bunch. What this does mean is that all of those personal encounters are validated online – friendships are documented and digitally displayed out of the necessity of their geographic separation. The minor league doesn't exclusively exist on the internet – that's just where its participants keep tabs.

The mass of attention young artists are currently capable of receiving online is in many ways based on an error in their own perception of similarity between each other. There is now a tenuous union among "internet artists" that totalizes the diverse efforts of many into a single hegemonic block of viewership through the networked links of aforementioned Web 2.0 platforms. To go through, person by person, the full list of participants in a BYOB exhibition would reveal a great diversity of methods and interests. Because this is a generation largely unwilling to concretely contextualize themselves through artist statements or text of any kind, the lowest common denominators of their mutual existence (youth, cultural fluency and social relations) remain the unstated bonds that tie artists of often greatly differing interests together. In *The Language of New Media*, Lev Manovich notes, "the popular understanding of new media identifies it with the use of a computer for distribution and exhibition rather than [as a site of] production." [1] In this way, many Web 2.0 artists have confused content and carrier – thinking of 'the internet' as a shared concern and not a shared platform for their diverse range of presumed intentions.

Perhaps this false perception of unity is due to a lack of critical writing surrounding internet art. While there are a growing number of artists online, there is not a proportionate number of media outlets dedicated to covering the efforts of this mass. The majority of coverage the minor league receives is from itself, as participants constantly link peers to other peers' work. The influential and widely read online publications covering internet art now surmount to a grand total of two; *Rhizome* and *Art Fag City*. Despite the courage of these sources to engage a relatively new art phenomenon, each falls short of being a definitive source for information regarding the minor league. While *Rhizome*'s blog has long been judged for being American-centric and uncritical, *Art Fag City*'s critical mentions of internet art rarely extend beyond a single (often snarky) paragraph. The most rigorous and intelligent critical writing on the work of Web 2.0 artists and their predecessors came from Gene McHugh's now-defunct blog, *Post Internet*, a resource that will likely be a defining historical record for this generation.

It simply asks too much to expect an evolved discourse from two media sources alone. What is hegemonic about internet art's peer viewership poses a chicken or egg question of origin in relation to the minor league's limitedly available media coverage.

Also necessary to remember is that the influx of participants in the minor league are typically very young – roughly 18-26 years old. It often takes much longer to gain a critical voice and the faculties necessary to begin feeling comfortable writing. The current period of internet art is marked by a lag in the number of people capable of starting a Tumblr (all) and the number of people who have studied the subjects necessary to provide an erudite judgment of those Tumblrs' conceptual content (few). Without this criticality, the minor league will continue to run based on what is commonly trafficked instead of what is critically validated – in addition to the fact that traffic itself will continue to flow to artistic subjects that are the most aesthetically common instead of those that are the most theoretically advanced or well understood.

It is not out of academic elitism that I bemoan the absence of critical voices for internet art – in fact, it's the complete opposite. I accept the idea that an aesthetic consensus is as valuable as an intellectual one. I also value the decentralized network of influence that Web 2.0 artists have created as a profoundly egalitarian step forward in artists' self-organization. But any proponent of pluralism must believe it best for there to be a wide-ranging and equally competing number of influences for our perception of work created in the minor league – to include the diversification of blogs and fostering of other modes of community-driven discourse. By its definition, pluralism is a tendency that runs contrary to all forms of monopolization – even that of the democratic majority. A minor league wholly determined by the reblogs of peers or the fleeting mention in only two viable media sources is no less tyrannical than a Greenbergian state of critical omnipotence.

The minor league would do well to take a page out of Conceptual Art's history book. In the late 60's and early 70's, one couldn't throw a rock without hitting the conceptual artists' new essays explaining their work and the movement they belonged to. This was because, in the absence of a theoretical discourse explaining the new form of art they were producing, conceptual artists needed to create the ground underneath their own feet through writing. A similar fervor must be initialized to help explain what this world of internet art is by its own participants – this essay will certainly fall short of that in numerous ways. Assuredly, history will be indifferent to these artists' Google Analytics or Tumblarity stats. With such a limited amount of articulation, the minor league sadly fails to know itself in the moment of its own existence. Cycles of repetition are only broken through decisive measures and risky proclamations. What a shame it would be, to see the efforts of hundreds of artists more equipped for communication than any generation before them, be forgotten because they never attempted to define themselves.

Regardless of this lag between those capable (or willing) to write about the minor league and those producing the art within it, I believe what is socially unified now among the minor league's artists will become increasingly splintered later for two reasons. The first is an issue of sheer quantity. Regarding the number of people now making art online, a pioneering internet artist once told me, "I remember when we all knew each other, or at least knew each other's names. It's nothing like that anymore." As the number of internet art participants dramatically increases so too will the filtration methods that define flows of traffic. What was originally conceived as the internet's greatest structural error in the 1990's was the 'Babel problem' – the idea that if everyone was talking, blogging, or sharing content no one would have time to listen. This problem was quickly nixed by a huge number of link aggregating websites that were visited based on their continued ability to share pre-filtered information that met their viewers' standard of interest. This is why VVORK gets more daily traffic than most individual artists I know combined. Promotional blogs providing links to minor league artists will continue to display *difference* among artists because it is in their best interest to define their form of taste-making as separate from other competing aggregates. If the minor league is not separated through its own written assertions or the variably negative and/or constructive criticism of journalistic media sources, it will surely be divided by the positive promotional attention of blogs looking to categorize the artistic content they share.

The second reason for the immanent 'split' of the minor league as a homogenous block of peers is an issue of capitalism and self-design. While free-labor communities, like Flickr's photographers, tend to unite around the similarities they find between each other, the free market rewards the *differentiation* of products available. Simply because galleries and museums are willing to hear out what wisdom the minor league's crowd may provide doesn't mean the entire crowd will be invited along for an exhibit. This is to say that if the minor league continues to place people in the major league we will see many more artists considering the formation of their interests in opposition to what is digitally common. Additionally, an increased awareness of the minor league and how it works will lead to a rise in artists who are able to translate their digital work into a physical manifestation, or as a distinct form of property in some regard. The most sophisticated participants in this group recognize their digital locale not as a final destination, but as one of many contexts to be inhabited. Successful minor league artists like Kari Altmann, Oliver Laric, AIDS-3D and Joel Holmberg have all embraced the production and display of objects since their late 2000's success. Even popular minor league artists whose projects primarily remain digital, like Rafael Rozendaal, have figured out a way to turn the boundless information they present online into a form of property through the sale of URLs to collectors. As with the creation of all new 'leagues', there will undoubtedly be a procession of new teams and athletic methods for success. Let the games begin.

2010. Originally published on *Image Conscious*.

[1] Lev Manovich, *The Language of New Media*, The MIT Press, Cambridge 2002, p. 19.

The Wealth of Pointlessness

I really started skateboarding in 6th grade. Previously, my mom's boyfriend's son Brian introduced me to it in 5th grade and on the weekends when I would go to his house, we would skateboard in his garage during the winter cold. I'm sure my pubescent bonding with Brian had a lot to do with taking up skateboarding, but I also remember 6th grade was the year recess stopped, leaving the enforced plans of a middle school gym teacher in its place. The school joke "What's your favorite class?" to which the student responds "Recess", is actually true for most kids not because they hate formal learning, but because they appreciate informal exploration and physical activity. Recess – more than art or music classes – is the pinnacle of creative and social opportunity an elementary student has all day and it was gone before I could even appreciate it. Damn.

'Playing' infers an action where the results of doing so are not entirely known in advance, where the objective of engaging in such an action is often found in the process of doing so or never firmly settled on at all. Children are usually the only people brave enough to play. Even the possibility of pointlessness drives adults crazy. Religions function to remove the burden of believing life is not infinite, circumventing the supposed pointlessness of living if you can't do it forever. Nationalities are inexplicably driven by a sense of collective *purpose*, as though each citizen of a given country was born there intentionally. Economic ideologies from capitalism to Marxism are ordered by how to best regiment productivity in labor. The idea of wasting time deathly scares people, so we have produced an increasingly intricate network of rituals, governments, cultures, laws, jobs, spiritual beliefs and more to make our progress as a species clearly apparent to us while we participate in it. According to our ability to fulfill, repeat, and expand on the network of activities and thoughts that keep us so expectedly busy, we are able to safely say what we all long to believe: *things are getting better*. The technological prowess of the great man-made wonders of the ancient world baffle us not for their results alone, but for the threat those results pose to the linear chronology of human progress. How is it possible that thousands of years ago we could have been smarter than we are now? In a world of outlawed pointlessness, artifacts like the Mayan ruins stand as a rip in the fabric of time itself.

How a person plays says a lot about her and sports are a convenient thing to do at recess. Sports provide firm objectives for success and a clear organization of time. Contained courts and fields, first quarter, half time, points compared, game over. Though sports are not as productive in a utilitarian sense as, say, building a house, they serve as a contained example of how the real world works in that some combination of talent, effort, and luck often determine one's ability to succeed. The most interesting moments in sports history arise from athletes who operate at the boundaries of rule making or athletic possibility. The NBA changed its policy on slam dunking due to the vertical dominance of Kareem Abdul-Jabar. Since readmitting the slam dunk in 1976 as a legitimate way to score points, time after time backboards have been shattered by this seemingly positive, point-scoring act. Baseball has been thrown into the spotlight the past 10 years due to rampant steroid use among players who want to hit more home runs and win more games. Wrestlers, horse jockeys, and runners of all kinds starve themselves to death to gain a competitive edge. The machine rages against itself.

Tim Berners-Lee, upon inventing the HTML structure that came to define the internet once remarked on it, "We knew we had invented a solution, now it was a matter of finding the problems it could solve." Play operates on a similarly reversed paradigm; the solution (free time) has been found, now it is a matter of figuring out what to do with it. In capitalist society, the hope for free time is a kind of Ponzi scheme. You work so that you may eventually not work, though if you continue to work through your own free time, there is a possibility that you may be able to cease working even sooner in life than you anticipated. This continual substitution of free time for labor leads many to working their entire lives. Having spent some 50 years in a non-stop state of labor, some people even refuse available free time and go back to their previous job. The tiring, though steady, re-enforcement of compensation, ordained responsibility, and familiar social interactions proves more desirable to those who, for the first time since high school or earlier, are presented with the bewildering freedom of formulating how to *play* late in their life. Throughout this process, free time becomes a paradox: it is both the enemy and the objective of marketplace productivity.

This is an unfortunate position for something so important as play to be in. The adult world's adversarial relationship with play, and the corresponding loss of chance encounter, non-linear thought, and creative discovery threaten to strip humanity of the traits that have provided our cultural, technological and social histories with happiness and depth. Such notions of progress have lead to lives more like the machines that were supposed to free us – we are shooting ourselves in the foot. Then again, maybe shooting yourself in the foot would be a good idea. Pain, joy and an ability to learn from mistakes are a few of the features that have separated us from the machines we employ.

Street skateboarding is a product of free time, it's a way adults and children play. Even the most utilitarian aspect of skateboards – their ability to serve as transportation – is ultimately not so utilitarian. Skateboards can usually only be ridden on paved planes while feet can travel across many different surfaces. Bikes can go faster than skateboards and cars even faster yet. Street skateboarding doesn't inherently operate according to teams, points, or seasons. It is an activity that has very few answers but offers many questions. The first question posed is to every publicly accessible surface, obstacle, object, and environment of the outside world: *How can I use you in harmony with my body and board?* 'Use' is the operative word here, as the practice of street skateboarding shares far more in common with Guy Debord's *détournement* than Marcel Duchamp's *readymade*. The street skateboarder does not point, collect or contextualize but instead uses, re-patterns and adapts.

There is little that is materially precious to the street skateboarder. To break one's own board is viewed as a kind of sacrifice to the joyful history that board previously brought or held as future potential. Countless waxed ledges and curbs have crumbled under the weight of human bodies hurling themselves down them time and again. The spots a street skateboarder visits come and go; some are materially altered to be uninhabitable by property owners and others become monitored by security forces. The street skateboarder lives in public, owning none of the architecture she inhabits. Nothing public is permanent, further enforcing the necessity of street skateboarders to find increasingly imaginative uses for their bodies and boards. A machine that never came with instructions cannot rage against itself, it can only find new ways to be built in the first place.

What is punk about street skateboarding is what is Situationist about punk. Basking in the decay of architecture and infrastructure, street skateboarding proposes no monument should exist forever anyway. For this reason, half pipe vert skateboarding (unlike the backyard pools California radicals of the 1970's snuck into and shredded) was always the antithesis of street skateboarding. Half pipes necessitated property ownership, granted access and/or the timely construction of ramps that would compel a body's ongoing motion. When the whole world is viewed as a skatepark, the monotony of a single, uniform ramp structure seems like an inhibition on the freedom skateboarding allows.

Vert is not the only enemy of street skateboarding's punk ethic of do it yourself use and discovery. Landing tricks should not be seen as the sole objective of skateboarding, even though landing a trick stands as a hyperbolic example of just how 'successful' an alternate use of a given object may be. Instead, the act of taking on an increasingly diverse array of public objects for the purpose of re-patterning their use is the logical ideal of an activity born from play. This means to foster a culture of *what can we try* instead of what can we 'land'. The binary of success versus failure suggests there was a point to rotating a piece of wood under your feet 360° in the first place. I am for a practice of skateboarding where tricks are routinely not landed, where momentum is jerky and discontinuous, where objects are grinded for the sake of being touched. Punks weren't perfectionists.

Similarly, today's orthodoxy of constantly filming threatens what is beautiful about skateboarding. This never-turn-the-camera-off tendency reveals an overwhelming urge to collect and own the act of play, to reclaim ephemeral moments through time rather than space. Perhaps street skateboarding's most advanced re-patterning was to become a sport. Maybe this incarnation of play is its most absurd realization possible; by becoming its own functional opposite skateboarding has truly investigated the conceptual terrain of all that it can be. Unfortunately, the popular potential of one vision for skateboarding (as a competitive sport) threatens to remove all chances for it to be understood as play by instituting a regime of contracts, sponsorships, professionalized labor, and all the rest that comes with athletics. Embracing pointlessness, error, and chance are the only ways to retake skateboarding from such a fate. If fun can't be had without rules, we might as well call it game over.

2011. Originally published in *YA5 Magazine*.

Friend Request From My Mom

We should probably start awarding Oscar recipients on a daily basis. Away from movie sets, every day, there are millions of people effortlessly gliding between multiple real life roles in a manner so convincing even they themselves believe their own performances as being true, all before assuming the next of their many different characters. What is it that allows a person to be a mother, sister, daughter, friend, and colleague all in the span of a few moments? Perhaps it's the same minor amnesia that rids us of our everyday memories for the sake of being able to move forward. This is what makes performing the easiest – to forget you're doing it in the first place.

Private conversation allows us to cater our speech to whomever we're addressing and mirror that person's behavior for optimal communication. This may be why so many have a fear of public speaking; without being able to target the communicative patterns of a single or a few people, we are left attempting to accommodate the 'average' audience member – a calculation that increases with difficulty the greater the number of people there are looking on. I tend to view these situations with an ignorance-is-bliss approach. If I don't know exactly who all I'm speaking to, I should grant myself the serenity of believing there is no way I can address everyone simultaneously. It's this way of thinking that lead me to a paranoiac state every time I logged on to Facebook.

The problem is, I *do* know the majority of my audience there. Laid out before me on my Facebook wall is a multiplicity of humors, conversational (in)formalities, political (dis)interests, and art knowledges that provide the diversity of my social life. But they also act as a foil to a complicated realization: in mirroring them, I too possess all of these other people's traits. To some degree, I *am* all of these other people. Any confusion over what group of friends a status update is addressed towards is simultaneously a confusion over what person I will choose to be online that day.

Back then, the only way I could come to terms with this situation was to empower myself with some kind of post-modern tactical resistance. Instead of being a confused schizophrenic burdened by the realization that I wasn't a single person anymore, I became strengthened through self-awareness of my identities – a master, instead of slave, to my own ability to socially perform a variety of characters. Maybe this kind of online self-design goes without saying – awareness of social multiplicity could be an ancient necessity buried under my generation's digital fetishes and obsessions with individuality. Even Facebook's design anticipates such awareness, allowing users privacy settings and network memberships to be able to speak to specific peers, to be specific people when we want to be.

Like a self-empowered stripper, digital self-design often requires the actor to believe her own intentionality or awareness eclipses that of those surrounding her. The only way to say that you are not singularly the person your best friend knows you as is to believe you are in a privileged position of knowing yourself in all of the roles your life consists of even more articulately than her. To the extent that no one knows me as a teacher, student, and best friend all at the same time, I am in control of knowing and performing my selves better than any other. Back then I was feeling like I was the king of my world. Then I got a friend request from my mom.

There is usually some embarrassment attached to receiving communication from your family on the internet. This is often attributed to family members being technologically incompetent, but we are also to blame. The discomfort we feel from their requests to be part of our online social lives is not unlike the awkwardness of being walked in on as an adolescent creating an alternate universe with action figures alone in your room. "Aren't you too old to be playing make believe?", they'd say. Family, in their technological ignorance and absolute personal awareness of our unpolished youth, are the self-reflective cracks by which we are able to re-connect to ourselves in lieu of the digital artifices we've created. This is to say the downside of a belief in totalizing digital self-design is that it breeds a certain epistemological myopia, a belief in the self as the creator of the self. There is no argument that we, as people, are *externally* designed quite as literal as mentioning we are each the biological products of other people. There is no protological control quite as controlling as that of birth itself. Facebook may delete me, but I'm sure glad my parents didn't. Receiving a friend request from my mom traced the limits of my own self-influence, reminding me that for every show's cast there is always a producer. This was a valuable lesson, and a paradox that could be applied to so much of our online existence: we are both in control of our destinies and products of our environment at all times.

http://bradtroemel.com